First published 2011 by Spellmount,
an imprint of The History Press
The Mill, Brimscombe Port
Stroud, Gloucestershire, GL5 2QG
www.thehistorypress.co.uk

British Library Cataloguing in Publication Data.
A catalogue record for this book is available from the British Library.

ISBN 978 0 7524 6432 9

Typesetting and origination by The History Press
Printed in the EU for The History Press.

THE WAR IN THE PENINSULA

Lieutenant Robert Knowles

AND

RECOLLECTIONS OF THE STORMING OF THE CASTLE OF BADAJOS

Captain James MacCarthy

SPELLMOUNT

Contents

RECOLLECTIONS OF THE STORMING OF THE
CASTLE OF BADAJOS

THE WAR IN THE PENINSULA: SOME LETTERS OF A LANCASHIRE OFFICER

Lieutenant Robert Knowles

Of the 7th, or Royal Fusiliers, A Lancashire Officer

Introduction by Ian Fletcher

Introduction

The British Army had been fighting in the Iberian Peninsula for almost a year when nineteen-year-old Robert Knowles became a lieutenant in the Royal Lancashire Militia in July 1809. Born on 4 April 1790, Knowles joined the army at a time when Arthur Wellesley, commander-in-chief of the army in the Peninsula, was struggling to establish both himself and his army in Spain. After opening the campaign in August the previous year with two victories at Roliça and Vimeiro, Wellesley had been superseded by Sir Harry Burrard and Sir Hew Dalrymple who between them conspired to let the French off the hook, by allowing themselves to be drawn into a truce, the notorious Convention of Cintra. This particular arrangement allowed for the evacuation of all French troops in Portugal including those garrisoning the fortresses of Almeida and Elvas. It was the kind of agreement that would almost certainly – in part – be made today, as it freed Portugal from enemy troops without the loss of a single life. Otherwise, it is certain that hundreds would have become casualties on both sides had the British Army been forced to continue the fight both against the French field army, penned in by both the Tagus and the Atlantic, and against the strongly defended fortresses.

But if the British generals who signed the Convention thought it would prove to be an end to the French problem in Portugal they were sadly mistaken. True, it removed the invaders from the country but it caused a storm of protest and outrage in England.

Enemy armies – especially those of Napoleon Bonaparte – were there to be thrashed and driven into the sea, not given a lift home to France, which is what both Dalrymple and Burrard – and, to an extent, Wellesley himself – agreed to. Furthermore, the French were given this ride home in the ships of the Royal Navy. And if this was not bad enough they were allowed to retain virtually all of their accumulated plunder along with their arms and most of their equipment. Little wonder that the popular saying of the day was, 'Oh, Cintra, Britannia sickens at thy name.' The agreement which so outraged both the people and government in England was likewise criticised in Portugal, for although it had rid their country of the invaders, the negotiations had been conducted almost entirely without the input of the Portuguese authorities themselves who, one would imagine, would certainly have had their own ideas on how to treat the defeated enemy. The upshot was that Burrard and Dalrymple were recalled to face a Court of Inquiry, Wellesley having gone home on leave anyway. The British Army in the meantime fell under the command of Sir John Moore.

Moore's brave and well-intentioned but ultimately ill-fated Corunna campaign of 1808–09 not only resulted in his death at the Battle of Corunna, on 16 January 1809, but saw the British Army chased ignominiously from Spain by Marshal Soult, leaving around 10,000 British troops in Portugal under Sir John Craddock as our only presence in a country which was threatened once again by invading French forces. But all was not lost, for in April 1809 Sir Arthur Wellesley, acquitted of all charges arising from the Court of Inquiry, returned to command the British Army in Portugal and by the middle of the following month had swept the French from Portugal for a second time following his victory at Oporto on 12 May. Then, marching quickly southwards, he turned his attention to Marshal Victor, whose isolated force sat idly on the Tagus close to the Spanish town of Talavera where, on 27–28 July, Wellesley won a bloody and costly victory which won him the title of 'Wellington.'

Two days before the Battle of Talavera the new lieutenant in the Royal Lancashire Militia, Robert Knowles, was sitting in his quarters in Bristol, having travelled there by mail coach from Manchester. It was the start of two years with his regiment, during which he learned the basic rudiments of his profession, how to drill his men, the army system and, equally important, how to behave like a gentleman. Unfortunately, Knowles wrote no further letters – or if he did, they haven't survived – and thus all goes quiet for the next two years until May 1811, when Knowles joined the 7th (Royal) Fusiliers.

Robert Knowles' first letter home from his new quarters in Maidstone was written the month after his regiment had been involved in one of the bloodiest – if not *the* bloodiest – battle of the Peninsular War, Albuera. Fought on 16 May 1811, the battle saw numerous instances of individual and collective bravery, none more so than by Lieutenant Marthew Latham, of The Buffs, whose heroic defence of one of his regiment's colours cost him one of his arms and half of his face, and by Daniel Hoghton, who watched his brigade cut to pieces around him, and yet still found time to change from his green coat into his regimental scarlet coat whilst still sitting in the saddle, and whilst enemy grape and musket shot flew all round him until he was struck down and killed. Regimental traditions were won at Albuera. It was here that the 57th (East) Middlesex Regiment won its nickname, 'The Die Hards,' for whilst the men of the regiment stood in an ever-dwindling line, torn apart by enemy fire at point-blank range, its commanding officer, William Inglis, himself struck down by a grape shot in the chest, lay behind them, refusing to be carried from the field and shouting, 'Die hard, 57th! Die hard!' And so they did. Inglis survived but of the 647 officers and men of his regiment who marched onto the field that morning, only 219 marched off of it.

But despite the tremendous and legendary fight put up by the men of Colborne's, Hoghton's and Abercrombie's brigades, the battle would almost certainly have been lost had it not been for the intervention of Lowry Cole and Henry Hardinge who, having seen the Allied commander, Marshal William Beresford, paralysed by indecision, took it upon themselves to launch the 4th Division – or at least Cole's Brigade – against the French in an attempt to wrest the initiative from the French. The ensuing advance remains one of the great moments in British military history as the Fusilier Brigade, consisting of two battalions of the 7th (Royal Fusiliers), and the 23rd (Royal Welsh) Fusiliers, supported by the Loyal Lusitanian Legion and the 11th and 23rd Portuguese, advanced into the maelstrom to turn the tide in the favour of the Allies. 'Nothing could stop that astonishing infantry,' wrote William Napier, the great historian of the war, and he was right. Nothing could, certainly not the French, and the Fusiliers stopped only after they stood bloodied and battered but triumphant on 'that fatal hill.'

The news of the bloodbath at Albuera reached Maidstone just before 29 June 1811, for Knowles mentions it in a letter to his brother. Just how much of the gory details of the battle had been publicly circulated at this time is unknown. Certainly, it was too early for eye-witness accounts to have filtered through into the public domain. However, enough of the battle was known to have caused wild rumours to be circulated, for Knowles writes of a rumour claiming that Wellington (who was not even present at Albuera) had lost a leg, and that Beresford had been killed (given the British losses and the severity of the action, the blame for which can be squarely laid at Beresford's feet, there were some who would later claim that the death of Beresford would not have been a bad thing!). As Knowles' descendant writes, 'Rumour and false intelligence were very prevalent in those days.' They certainly were.

Robert Knowles can consider himself lucky he was not at Albuera, otherwise he may well have been amongst the 706 casualties which the two battalions of the 7th suffered during the battle. Nevertheless, he was to see some bitter fighting himself during the two years he was in the Peninsula. He arrived in Lisbon in August 1811, at a time when, after a year of manoeuvring and countering, and after some hard fighting (in addition to Albuera, Wellington had just about overcome Marshal Massena at Fuentes de Onoro on 3–5 May and had himself failed to take the fortress of Badajoz the following month) Wellington's army had settled down into positions on the Caia river to the south-west of Ciudad Rodrigo, the fortress that commanded the northern corridor between Spain and Portugal, waiting for an opportunity to attack.

During late September 1811, there were several clashes between Wellington and the French in front of Fuenteguinaldo, Wellington's headquarters, the most famous of which came on 25 September at El Bodon, where the cavalry of the King's German Legion, supported by British cavalry and infantry – in particular the 5th (Northumberland) Fusiliers – performed heroics against a vastly superior French cavalry force. Knowles himself saw action two days later, at Aldea da Ponte, his first smell of powder in the Peninsula.

By the end of the year Wellington had moved farther north as he turned his attention towards Ciudad Rodrigo. Four companies of the 7th Fusiliers, including Knowles, were despatched to the north of the fortress, to the small village of Barba del Puerco, which overlooks the river Agueda and the only bridge over the river north of Ciudad Rodrigo. One can almost see him and his comrades, standing on the vast, flat rocks, gazing down into the immense gorge at the great Roman bridge that spans the roaring waters of the Agueda. On 19 January 1812 Ciudad Rodrigo was stormed by the 3rd and Light Divisions. Knowles himself worked hard in the miserable, cold trenches before the town, undertaking 24-hour shifts, but he was disappointed when his division was relieved by the 3rd Division on

19 January for it meant that he was denied the opportunity of taking part in the storming. Knowles was not to wait for too long before he had another chance to take part in a storming, for barely two months after the capture of Ciudad Rodrigo, Wellington's men were back in the south, and were positioned in front of the tremendously strong walls of the fortress of Badajoz, which commanded the southern corridor between Spain and Portugal. The fortress had denied Wellington in June 1811 and, indeed, ever since 1809 when British troops wounded at Talavera were left in the town, only to be poorly cared for by the people – known to be pro-French – the place had attracted a very bad reputation amongst Wellington's men. Their feelings were amply summed up by Lieutenant William Grattan, soon to be wounded during the storming, who wrote, 'In a word, the capture of Badajoz had long been their [the British] idol; many causes led to this wish on their part; the two previous unsuccessful sieges, and the failure of the attack against San Christobal in the latter; but above all, the well-known hostility of its inhabitants to the British army, and, perhaps might be added, a desire for plunder which the sacking of Rodrigo had given them a taste for. Badajoz was, therefore, denounced as a place to be made example of; and unquestionably no city, Jerusalem exempted, was ever more strictly visited to the letter than was this ill-fated town.'

And so it was, for on the momentous night of 6 April 1812 the fortress of Badajoz was assaulted by the full force of Wellington's army. Attacks were made on the three breaches made in the walls, whilst two other attacks were made by escalade at the castle and on the San Vicente bastion. Knowles himself was fortunate that he was spared the horror of the assaults on the breaches, for his regiment was ordered to attack the Fort San Roque, 200 yards or so outside the walls of the town. It was here that the French had constructed a dam which caused the forming of an inundation or false lake in front of the breaches, something which caused the stormers so many problems. In the event, Knowles was lucky to escape with nothing more than a badly wounded hand when a piece of grape shot dashed his sword into pieces. 'I providentially escaped without any serious injury, although my clothes were torn from my back,' he wrote, adding, 'My sword hand is much cut and bruised, which accounts for my bad writing, and my right side is a little bruised.'

Wellington's infantry made over forty separate attacks on the breaches, and forty times they were driven back by a very tenacious garrison commanded by Baron Armand Phillipon. His efforts were ultimately in vain, however, for the two attacks by escalade, intended to be simply diversionary attacks, succeeded and the town was won at last. But at what a cost! Nearly 3,500 men were killed or wounded during the storming, and these concentrated into two small areas in front of the breaches and at the foot of the castle walls. Little wonder, therefore, that Wellington broke down and wept when he saw the devastation at the breaches on the morning of 7 April. By then, of course, Wellington's vengeful troops, driven to the point of madness by the fury of their assaults, were well and truly engaged on an orgy of pillage, murder, drunkenness and destruction. And well earned it was too, they would say, for the French had defied convention and had refused to surrender even though practical breaches had been made in the walls of the town. Seventy-two hours later, the disorder, 'subsided, rather than was quelled,' and the dazed and exhausted British troops staggered away, laden with plunder and with mightily-sore heads, but triumphant, having presented Wellington with the second of the 'keys to Spain.' [A more expansive introduction to the siege is of course provided in the introduction to Captain MacCarthy's memoir that follows, though it was thought that this brief analysis should stand for sake of continuity.]

A threat by Marshal Marmont to Ciudad Rodrigo caused Wellington to return north, rather than head east along the valley of the Tagus towards Madrid, the logical route. The threat was averted and, in June 1812, Wellington was on the march northeast towards Salamanca, the beautiful university town, and a great base for the French armies in central Spain. After weeks of manoeuvring the two armies finally fell in with each other and by the afternoon of 22 July were face to face looking out across the great, dusty plain to the south of the small village of Los Arapile. Unfortunately for the French, a combination of a lapse in concentration and overconfidence, led to their army becoming over-extended, something which Wellington was quick to seize upon. By the end of the day the Allies had completely smashed Marmont's army, and it was only the unauthorised withdrawal by Carlos d'Espana of Spanish troops guarding the bridge over the River Tormes at Alba de Tormes, which allowed the French to make good their escape and take the shine off what was otherwise a crushing victory for Wellington.

Salamanca also saw Robert Knowles receive his second wound of the war. And a far more serious one it might have been if the musket ball which struck him in the arm had hit home with more force than it did. 'I had it cut out the same night,' he wrote, 'and I believe the bone is not injured.'

Knowles was lucky, for in 1812 the usual course for surgeons presented with broken bones resulting from gunshot wounds was to reach for the amputating saw. Despite playing down his wound, Knowles was listed as severely wounded, whilst he also suffered from 'fever and ague' as well as what he called, 'a most severe bowel complaint.' He also complained – as did most of Wellington's officers – of a lack of funds, the army being almost permanently in a state of arrears of pay. Indeed, it was a sorry thing for an officer to be without money whilst on campaign and Knowles is certainly not alone in writing home about the problem.

1812 ended in massive frustration and disappointment for Wellington. Despite all of the triumphs – Ciudad Rodrigo, Badajoz, Salamanca and the occupation of Madrid – he ended the year where he began; back in Portugal. After his army had marched into Madrid on 12 August he took himself off to lay siege to Burgos, a siege that went disastrously wrong from the outset. With too few troops, and even fewer heavy guns, the siege staggered on through September and October until by the 22nd of that month, with French forces gathering to the north, Wellington was forced into an ignominious withdrawal. The weather turned against him, the commissariat broke down, the discipline of many of the troops dissolved and the whole episode turned into a repeat – some say worse – of the retreat to Corunna.

Knowles was spared the rigours of the retreat owing to his detachment to the regimental depot at Santarem, on the Tagus, north of Lisbon. Unfortunately, there is only a single letter from here, in which Knowles at least had the satisfaction of enjoying an increase in pay owing to a staff appointment. The letter to his Father, written in February 1813, is, sadly, the last. By the spring of 1813 Wellington had crossed the border into Spain once again, embarking upon his final – and decisive –campaign. On 21 June he crushed the French at Vittoria, a victory which effectively spelled the end of French ambitions in the Peninsula. The victory opened up the way for an invasion of France itself and the following month Wellington had driven the French back over the Pyrenees. But the French were not giving up without a fight. Indeed, on 25 July they launched an offensive against the passes at Maya and Roncesvalles in an attempt to drive through to the beleaguered French garrison of Pamplona. It was during this fighting – the battles between 25 July and 2 August subsequently became known as the Battle of the Pyrenees – that Robert Knowles was killed.

The pass of Roncesvalles, once held centuries before by the immortal Roland against the Basque hordes, is marked by two massive hills to the east and west. The French attacks to the east were held back for around four hours by a few hundred light infantrymen ensconced in some rocks before the pressure told and they were pulled back. On the western side of the pass, on the Linduz Plateau, General Ross – soon to fall at Bladensburg – led his brigade up to face the French under General Reille. It was a fierce fight, Major Tovey's company of the 20th Regiment getting stuck into the enemy with their bayonets, with Tovey himself crying, 'Bayonet away! Bayonet away!' Into the fray were thrust the 7th Fusiliers, Knowles amongst them. We are not sure how he died, but somewhere up on that narrow path, overlooking the magnificent scenery of both France and Spain, Knowles met his death, the only officer of the Fusiliers to be killed during the battle.

Robert Knowles still lies somewhere up on the Linduz Plateau today. The British troops were driven off by Reille's men who would – hopefully – have buried Knowles, along with their own casualties. There was certainly no chance for the British to undertake the task. If he wasn't buried by the French, it would have been a good few days before the British returned. At Maya, fought on the same day as Roncesvalles, the British dead lay exposed both to the elements and to wild animals and were interred by their comrades when they returned a week or two after the fight.

Knowles was no different from hundreds of other British officers who died in the line of fire whilst on active service in the Peninsula. Ralph Bunbury, of the 95th was the first, killed at Obidos on 15 August 1808. The last died at Bayonne on 14 April 1814. It is fortunate, however, that his memory lives on, not only in the memorial in his church at St Peter, Bolton-le-Moore, in Lancashire, but in these letters.

Opposite: Title page of the 1913 edition of Captain Knowles' memoir.

THE WAR IN THE PENINSULA

PENINSULA

SOME LETTERS

OF

LIEUTENANT ROBERT KNOWLES,

Of the 7th, or Royal, Fusiliers,
A Lancashire Officer.

Arranged and Annotated by his Great-Great-Nephew

SIR LEES KNOWLES, BARONET,

C.V.O., D.L.

JULY 25th, 1913.

Preface

The following lines are from a letter, dated 28 June 1913, written by Professor C. W. C. Oman, M.A., of All Souls College, Professor of Modern History (Chichele) in Oxford University:—

'I rejoice to see that there is to be a second edition of these interesting letters, which contain not only a record of the daily life of the 4th Division, with all the details of its toils and marches, but several pieces of narrative of real historical value, especially with regard to the fights at Albuera, Aldea da Ponte, and Salamanca. The writer was a keen and intelligent young soldier, and his letters have not only a special interest for those who are connected with the old 7th, the Royal Fusiliers, but also much that all who care to know about the British Army in the Peninsula will be glad to read.'

Introduction to
the 1913 Edition

These letters were written a hundred years ago by my great-great-uncle, Lieutenant Robert Knowles, and I believe that they, and the notes of Sergeant John Spencer Cooper, are the only contemporary regimental record of the 7th, or Royal, Fusiliers. They came into the possession of his niece, Margaret Mary Knowles, a daughter of James Knowles, who was Town Clerk of Bolton. They were lent years ago to my father, and he made a copy of them. In 1890, I compared the copy with the originals, which were in a fragile state – moreover, some of them were missing – and this reproduction is from a copy which I made at the time of the comparison. Some of the original letters are again before me. The handwriting shows considerable care, and it is very different from what one would expect in letters written during a campaign. The letters are printed here in their entirety, and the original spelling has been retained. Each letter is folded twice, in long strips, the creases being at right angles to the writing, and the ends of the strips folded together, and sealed in the middle as a rule with red sealing-wax, in several instances bearing, from the impress of a military button, a rose with the legend round it, *Honi soit qui mal y pense.* The address is lengthwise on the back of the sheet. On the letter of 7 July 1811, is printed in red, square, straight letters, 'Maidstone.'

On the letter of 29 August 1811, is the circular postmark, 'Portsmouth, 1 Oc. 1. 1811. 73.'; on the letter of 5 November 1811, is the postmark, 'Lisbon, De. 13. 1811. F.'; on the letter of 31 December 1811, is the postmark, 'Lisbon, Ja. 22. 1812'; on the letter of 20 January 1812, is the postmark, 'Lisbon, Feb. 18. 1812'; and, on the letter of 23 September 1812, is the postmark, 'Lisbon, Se. 23. 1812.' On several letters, printed in black, is the expression 'Packet Letter,' with a town after it, such as 'Plymouth,' and several of them have '2/5' written upon the face of them. The letter of the Duke of Wellington bears the old blue twopenny stamp, and it is sealed with his crest surrounded by the garter and surmounted by a coronet.

The first of the six volumes of the History of the War in the Peninsula and in the South of France, from the year 1807 to the year 1814, by Major-General Sir William F. P. Napier, K.C.B., Colonel 27th Regiment, contains the story of the first portion of the war ending in May 1809, just two months earlier than the first of the letters hereafter printed. That History, full of glowing language and brilliant description, and the admirable, carefully-balanced, and probably more accurate History of the War by Professor Oman, contain all that is essential in connection with this glorious epoch of British military history. The treaty of Tilsit had given Napoleon a commanding position in Europe, and had brought him directly into conflict with England. France and England were both strong, but the battle of Trafalgar had prevented the invasion of England, and Napoleon therefore proposed to weaken her naval and commercial strength by barring the Continent against English manufactures. It was necessary to do this by French troops. Portugal was virtually an unguarded province of England, whence, and from Gibraltar, English goods passed into Spain. To check this traffic by force was not easy. Spain was to France nearly what Portugal was to England, and the French cause was therefore popular in Spain, and the weak Court of Spain was subservient. Napoleon, accordingly, proposed to place his brother, Joseph Bonaparte, then King of Naples, upon the Spanish Throne, and eventually on 24 July 1808, he was proclaimed King of Spain and the Indies, becoming, however, the object of a nation's hatred. The volume deals with the principal operations in the Eastern and Central Provinces, and, having shown that the Spaniards, however restless, were unable to throw off the yoke, the writer turns to Portugal, where the invasion was first stayed, and finally forced back by greater strength.

L. K.

JULY 25TH, 1913.

The War in the Peninsula and the Story of a Lancashire Officer

Old letters, more than old books bring us into direct contact with men of a past age. As we read their exact words and see their handwriting we seem to know them, and they become real living beings and not figures of imagination, however powerfully portrayed. With soldiers, taking into consideration men of action in every sphere of public life, this is perhaps more true than with any other class, as their work in the world is necessarily more arresting, more striking, more immediately effective.

In these letters, we have an account of stirring events, written within a few days of their occurrence by a young officer who had himself taken part in them. He gives his experiences and impressions modestly, and like most British officers, he is under, rather than over the mark, in stating their value where his own deeds are concerned. When he tells his father that his wounds are slight, the despatches say 'severe.' His description of the sufferings of the sick and wounded after Salamanca is not as painful reading as those of the historians who have examined every particle of evidence. The statements made in these letters bear the test of comparison with the official reports, contemporary letters and narratives. As we read, we feel that we are in touch with a man of knowledge, and a soldier, whose patriotism took him into the battlefield. He had not the inducement of monetary reward; for, after the manner of his kind, he had to pay, and pay heavily, to serve his country.

Such an example should not be forgotten, or the memory of heroism and of self-sacrifice be buried in oblivion. For a well-informed, patriotic, nation, time brightens rather than dims the lustre of the fame of soldiers who have fallen in battle, and the glories of the War in the Peninsula have been revived by the series of centenaries that have been celebrated since 1908. A nation or country forgetful of its past history is one that is doomed to defeat and decay.

1809

The year 1809 opened badly for England. An illustrious soldier was struck down in the very moment of his victory. Sir John Moore had led the army committed to his care with consummate skill. His retreat on Corunna accomplished its purpose, and justified his foresight. The Emperor Napoleon at the head of his hitherto victorious legions was drawn from Madrid, whither fate decreed that he was never to return. The soldiers who fought under Moore returned to England worn out by privation and hardships. Within a few months they were again hastened to South Beveland on what was known as the Walcheren Expedition, and then, without accomplishing any useful purpose, they returned to England decimated by fever, many dying, and a large proportion of the survivors remaining for some years in a state of convalescence. Ireland at that time absorbed an Army of no less than 60,000 men. England was garrisoned largely by the constitutional force, the Militia. One regiment, the Royal Lancaster, was embodied and quartered at Bristol, and the writer of these letters joined it there in July 1809.

Robert Knowles was the fourth son of Robert Knowles, of Quarlton and Eagley Bank, Little Bolton, in the County of Lancaster. He was born on 4 April 1790, and in 1809 he was gazetted as Lieutenant in the Royal Lancaster Regiment.

The first letter to his father gives a glimpse of the old coaching-days, a journey of thirteen hours from Manchester to Birmingham, a crowded mail coach necessitating the delay of one night, and then an all-day journey to Bristol. The letter is dated Bristol, 25 July 1809, and the reader will notice the coincidence that the day was a fatal one for the writer.

To Mr. Robert Knowles.
Bristol, July 25th, 1809.

Dear Father,—I now sit down to inform you of my safe arrival at Bristol. I left Manchester at half-past one o'clock on Saturday morning, accompanied by Lieut. Bottomley, and we arrived at Birmingham at half-past two o'clock Saturday evening, from which town the mail was filled, so that we were obliged to stop one night at Birmingham. We immediately took seats in the stagecoach, which sets off early on Sunday morning, and arrived at this place at nine o'clock on Sunday evening. We had a very pleasant and agreeable journey. On Monday morning we waited upon the Colonel, and I delivered Capt. Mason's letter to his friend, Lieut. Bythesea, by whom I have been very handsomely received. He introduced me to the officers of the Regiment, who appear to be very agreeable gentlemen. Lieut. Bythesea's best respects to Capt. Mason, and please to inform him that he has a little boy. Please to return Capt. Mason my sincere thanks for the kindness shown unto me. Mr. Bottomley and myself have taken lodgings in College Place, which consists of two bedrooms and one parlour, for which we are to pay 21s. per week. Bristol is a very large and pleasant city, and the docks are full of shipping in consequence of the embargo. We have very bad news from abroad, but hope it will be better than what is represented. On Monday night there was a fatal duel in the French prison near this place between two of the prisoners. The weapons they fought with were two pieces of broken files, about six inches long, sharpened and tyed at the end of sticks. They fought a considerable time, when one of them was stuck to the heart. If you do see *Mr. Orrell desire him to join as soon as possible, as I think it would be much better for him, as he will have more to learn than he is aware of.

I will write again in the course of a week. I am very anxious to hear how my †Grandfather is, and I do hope this will find you and all the family in good health. Please to remember me to all enquiring friends. With the greatest affection and respect for you, my brothers, sisters, and all relations.—I subscribe myself,

Your affectionate Son,

R. Knowles.

P.S.—I hope you will not delay writing to me. Please to address—

Lieut. Knowles,

1st R.L. Militia,

Bristol.

In haste and a bad pen.

* Lieutenant Andrew Orrell.

†Andrew Knowles, of Quarlton, and of Eagley Bank, Little Bolton, the only surviving son of Robert Knowles: buried at Turton, 8 February 1810, aged 74: will dated 11 October 1809, proved at Chester, 25 August 1810.

There is here a long break of two years in the letters which have been preserved. The next is a short note from Hull, written on 25 May 1811, when the writer was in daily expectation of receiving a commission in the regular army.

> *To Mr. Robert Knowles.*
>
> Hull, 25th May, 1811.

Dear Father,—As I gave you reason to expect me at home about this time, I think it my duty to inform you that I cannot leave the Regiment until my name appears in the Gazette, which I hope will be in a few days, after which I will lose no time in repairing home. We have no news here worth committing to paper, particularly as I am very soon expecting to see you. Please to remember me to my sisters, brothers, and all enquiring friends.

Your affectionate Son.
(Name torn off.)

The 7th Royal Fusiliers

On 7 May 1811, Robert Knowles was appointed Lieutenant in the 7th Royal Fusiliers, then, as now, one of the most distinguished regiments in the army; and, within a month, he was at Maidstone where he had joined the Depot of his Regiment.

This letter tells the home-circle of his arrival, and gives some information about the uniform and expenses of those days. Six guineas for the stamp on a first commission was a heavy tax for a young officer. As is not even now-a-days unusual, the tailor came in for the chief share of the spoil, with a bill of £20 for a regimental coat and wings.

To Mr. Robert Knowles.

Maidstone, 23rd June, 1811.

Dear Father,—I arrived at London about ten o'clock on the evening of the 19th, and at Maidstone on the evening of the 21st, where I was well received by the commanding Depôt. There is a draft of four hundred men and nine officers (including myself) ordered to be in readiness to proceed to Portsmouth to embark for Portugal on the 25th inst., but we have not yet received our route, and I think it probable it will be put off a few days longer. I wish you to send me by the Defiance Coach from the Bridgewater Arms, Manchester, leaves at four o'clock in the evening, my large box (if it is yet arrived from Hull), with my two old regimental coats, white pantaloons, two pair blue pantaloons, the best I have got, two sashes, sword knot, cocked hat, shoes, pair of boots, linen, bed-linen, two black silk handkerchiefs, paper-case, and any other things that I have got which you think will be of use to me. I am very sorry I did not see my brother ★Chadwick at Manchester, and it hurt me much to leave my sister alone, but I hope she very soon found him. When we receive our route I will write you by that day's post. We are seven days' march from Portsmouth. I am going to London tomorrow to stop a few days, where I officer and officers of the Regiment at present with the intend providing myself with everything that is necessary. I am under the necessity of requesting you will send me £30 by return of

★ Third son of Robert Knowles, of Eagley Bank, Little Bolton: born 27 January and baptized at Bolton, 24 February 1786: died, unmarried 17 December 1817: buried at Turton.

post (underneath you have an estimate of my expenses), which I hope will be the last sum I shall trouble you for until my return from abroad. Please to remember me to my brothers, sisters, and all enquiring friends.

Your affectionate Son,

R. Knowles, Lt., Royal Fusiliers.

Estimate of my Expense: —	£	s.	d.
Regimental Coat and Wings	20	0	0
Sabre	4	4	0
Cap	6	6	0
Large Blue Pantaloons and Chain	2	5	0
Three Pair Shoes and Gaiters	2	14	0
Belt and Breast Plate	2	0	0
Commission	6	6	0
Plate			
Sundrys			
	£43	15	0

The above is the lowest estimate, and I am having my old coat cut down for a service jacket, which will be an expense of three or four pounds in gold lace, &c.

My address in London, where I shall remain until Saturday next:—
Lieut. Knowles, 7th Royal Fusiliers,
No. 28, Suffolk Street,
Charing Cross, London.

Directions for my large box:—
Lt. Knowles, 7th Royal Fusiliers, Maidstone, to be forwarded
by the coach from the Golden Cross, Charing Cross, London.

P.S.—If you can send my box by the Defiance Coach on
Thursday I shall receive it at London. In that case, direct it to
be left at the Coach Office till called for. Please mention the
direction in your letter, which I hope you will not fail to send
by return of post.

I intended writing yesterday, but there was no post from this
town with speed.

P.S.—I have this moment received a parcel from home, also a
letter from my brother. Therefore, it will be unnecessary sending me bed-linen or anything else, unless I find it necessary to
write for them when I get to Portsmouth, but I hope you will
not fail sending me the sum I have wrote for by return of post,
after seeing Capt. Robinson's letter.

~

Lieutenant Knowles was in London on 29 June 1811, and
the victory to which he refers in his letter of that date must
have been the Battle of Albuera, fought on 16 May. Marshal
Beresford, and not Wellington, commanded the Allies.

Rumour and false intelligence were very prevalent in those
days. The distance, the difficulties of communication, the
uncertainty of sailing-ships, the stories circulated by interested
parties, both friends and foes, all tended to create fiction, sometimes alarming, and often harassing.

To Mr. Chadwick Knowles.

London, June 29th, 1811.

Dear Brother,—I have just received yours of the 27th instant, enclosing a £30 draft and one pound note, for which I return my Father my sincere thanks. You have given me Mr. John Woods' address, but it was unnecessary, having called upon him twice, but have nothing to thank him for but mere civility. We have no further information respecting our march, but expect it daily. You mention my sister's letter that she wrote me. I shall take an opportunity of answering it in a few days. I intend returning to Maidstone on Monday next. I should have deferred writing until tomorrow, having received your letter so late in the evening, but for a report there is in Town that there has been a very severe action in Spain, in which our army was crowned with victory, but with very severe loss. Report says that Lord Wellington has lost a leg, and that Marshall Beresford is killed, but the French army is entirely dispersed. It is believed by many people in the Town, but I am very doubtful, as it is a French account, and it is unusual for them to spread reports to their disadvantage. I have not time to write anything more unless I lose the advantage of to-night's post.

Please to remember me to all our family and enquiring friends, and believe me,

Your affectionate Brother,

R. Knowles, Lt., Royal Fusiliers.

Excuse haste and a bad pen.

~

To his sister are given particulars of the final marching orders, and the keen spirit of the soldier is shown in his desire to take his place in the field against the enemies of his country.

Note.—This letter is sealed with red sealing-wax, bearing the impress of a button, on which is a central heraldic rose with the inscription round it of '*Honi soit qui mal y pense*', partly legible.

To Miss Knowles.
Maidstone, July 7th, 1811.

My dear Sister,—I received yours of the 20th ult. in due time, and am glad to see you give yourself credit for not opening my letters, but I still think that a female's curiosity will not be satisfied until she knows the contents. You say that you have heard a report that the officers of our Regiment are returning from Spain, but I am happy to inform you that there is not the least foundation for the report. So far from it that we nine officers and 400 men have received our route to march for Portsmouth on Wednesday and Thursday next, there to embark to join our gallant comrades in Spain. I am ordered to march with the 2nd Division on Thursday, and shall arrive at Portsmouth on Wednesday, the 17th instant, where I expect to hear from home on my arrival with a parcel containing the remainder of my shirts, night-shirts, stockings, bed-linen, military books, French books, brace of small pistols with the moulds, and portmanteaus. I am induced to write for those things, our Regiment having a store at Lisbon, where I intend leaving most of my baggage, as I can at any time send for everything that is necessary to that place. I spent my time very pleasantly in London, where I remained about eight days. I was in a private lodging-house along with an officer of our Regiment, who knows a great deal of the town, and he was so obliging as to go with me wherever I pleased. I wish you to forward the parcel by the coach on the 12th or 13th, with directions to be left till called for. Before I take leave of Old England I will write to my father, and every future opportunity that occurs I shall take great pleasure in writing to my friends in Lancashire. I shall endeavour to see Lieut. Woods in Spain; if his friends have anything to send to him I should be happy to take charge of it. Please to remember me to my father, brothers, sisters, and all enquiring friends, and believe me,

Your affectionate Brother,

Robt. Knowles, Lt.,

Royal Fusiliers.

P.S.—It is dinner-hour, therefore must conclude.★

~

A march of seven days brought Lieutenant Knowles and the detachment of the 7th Royal Fusiliers from Maidstone to Hilsea Barracks, Portsmouth, on 17 July 1811.
The embarkation took place on the following day. Adverse winds detained the fleet of transports for a week at Spithead, where the following letter was written on 24 July 1811:—

★This letter is also sealed.

To Mr. Robert Knowles.

Spithead, July 24th, 1811.

My dear Father,—I take the latest opportunity of addressing you on leaving for a short time my much-beloved
country. I must commence with our march from Maidstone
to Portsmouth, which was a very pleasant one. We passed
through Tunbridge, Tunbridge Wells, East Grinstead, Horsham,
Petworth, Chichester to Hilsea Barracks, near Portsmouth,
where we arrived on the 17th, and embarked early on the
morning of the 18th, in the Matilda Transport No. 68. We
immediately dropped down to Spithead, where we have since
remained, weather bound, but there is now a fair wind, and we
expect to sail in the course of the day. I have received a trunk
from home.

Inclosed I found a kind letter from you. My brother's letter
is also come to hand, in which he informs me that I might
expect to see Mr. Orrel (*sic*) in Portsmouth. He is arrived and
on board the Arethusa transport, but I have not yet seen him.
I went on board that vessel yesterday, but he was on shore. If
possible I will see him in the course of the day, as my brother
informs me he has a portmanteau in charge for me. There is a
large fleet of transports going to Portugal from this place, with
about three thousand troops on board. If we have a quick passage we shall be a very seasonable supply for Lord Wellington.
Our detachment is about 370 strong, in high spirits, and anxious to join their brave comrades in Spain. 27th.—The wind
is now fair, and the fleet is now getting under weigh. We have
no news, therefore must conclude. Trusting I shall have the

pleasure of seeing my dear father, brothers, and sisters all in good health on my return,

I remain, dear Father,

Your affectionate Son,

R. Knowles, Lt.,

Royal Fusiliers.

In haste.

P.S.—I have seen Mr. Orrel; he is in good health. I forgot to say that the wind changed on the 24th, therefore delayed finishing my letter for a few days. You shall hear from me on my arrival at Lisbon.

~

The Fleet was compelled to put into Falmouth, and the last letter he was fated to write within sight of his native land was written from the Cornish port. It is easy to imagine the impatience of 10 officers and 370 men, 'cabined, cribbed, confined,' for sixteen days in a sailing transport, between Spithead and Falmouth, with little comfort and indifferent food. Biscuit and salt beef was then the staple ration of our soldiers, and even that was not always in a sound and wholesome condition. In those days such meat, supplied for long voyages, was called 'junk,' because it resembled old rope-ends in hardness and toughness. But, there was in some measure compensation in a quick trip to Lisbon, as twelve days was good sailing in the early years of the nineteenth century.

To Mr. Robert Knowles.
Falmouth Harbour, Aug. 9th, 1811,
on board Matilda Transport.

Dear Father,—You will see in the public prints an account of our arrival at this place. We were obliged to put in by contrary winds on the morning of the 2nd inst. I have delayed writing, expecting hourly to set sail, when I hope we shall be more fortunate. The fleet for Lisbon consists of about seventy sail. We are on board the fastest sailer and the finest transport in the fleet. Contrary to my expectation I have not experienced the least sea-sickness, and I am happy to say our men continue in the best state of health. You will see in this month's Army list how fortunate I am in my appointment, as there are now eight lieuts. junior to me. I saw Mr. Orrel in Falmouth on Wednesday last. He told me that he had wrote home and mentioned that he had seen me. The last accounts from our Regiment, the 2nd Battalion were under orders for England, but I hope the orders will be countermanded. On my arrival in Portugal, I hope I shall have the pleasure of receiving a letter from you. Please to remember me to my brothers, sisters, and all enquiring friends, and believe me,

Your affectionate Son,

R. Knowles, Lt.,
Royal Fusiliers.

P.S.—We are now under sail. Adieu! Please to direct: Lt. Knowles, 7th Royal Fusiliers, with the Army in Portugal.

Two letters from Portugal describe the impression which Lisbon, the capital, made on the soldiers, upon their arrival there.

To Mr. Robert Knowles.
Lisbon, August 24th, 1811.

Dear Father,—I am happy to inform you of my arrival at this place on the 21st inst. We had a very good passage from Falmouth, and landed at Lisbon on the 22nd inst. Our men are quartered in the Convent of Carmo, but we expect daily to march to the Army. Our detachment was very fortunate in leaving England before the arrival of our 2nd Battalion, which has left Lisbon about three weeks. I was very sorry to see so many of our brave fellows sick and wounded in the hospitals at Lisbon and Belem. A great many of our officers are at Lisbon sick and wounded, many of them without hopes of recovery. A Lieut. Jones, of our Regiment, died yesterday. The last accounts from our Army they were blockading Ciudad Rodrigo—our Regiment is attached to the Light Division. To give you a description of Lisbon—the town is well built, and stands on the rise of a hill, but the streets smell abominably. The filthy inhabitants throw their dirt into the streets as soon as it is dark, and they pay little attention to clearing it away in the morning. I will return the letters for Lieut. Woods and Richard Booth, of the 48th Regiment, the first opportunity, understanding they have left this country for England. I will write to you as soon as we join the Regiment. I am informed that we are to march through the most barren country, laid waste by the army. We have no news here, and have not heard from England since our arrival. Be so good as to remember me to all enquiring friends, particularly to my dear sisters and brothers, and believe me,

Your affectionate Son,

R. Knowles, Lt.,
Royal Fusiliers.

P.S.—I am sorry I have delayed writing until half an hour before the sailing of the Packet, but lost no time in writing after receiving the information, therefore you must excuse all mistakes and the shortness of the letter. We are about 250 miles from the Army.

To Mr. Robert Knowles.

Lisbon, 29th August, 1811.

Dear Father,—I avail myself of this opportunity of forwarding the enclosed letters to Mr. Wood, understanding that both his son and Richard Booth are returned to England with the 2nd Battalion of the 48th. We embark to-morrow morning to sail up the Mondego as far as Coimbra, so that we shall be a few days at sea. I mentioned to you in my last letter that Lisbon is a dirty town; it is also infested with a multitude of dogs, which no person owns. On account of their infernal howling (all the night) I could not sleep for several nights after my arrival. I wrote in my last that our men were quartered in the Convent of Carmo. The officers are all billeted in private houses. We have our regular rations of beef and biscuits, but the meat we have is so poor that it would be burnt if exposed for sale in Bolton Market. At present we are in a town where there is plenty of good things. When we leave, John Bull must give up his idea of good living. I have not seen Mr. Orrel since my arrival in Lisbon, but hear that he marches in a few days to join his Regiment, which is with General Hill's Division near Badajos. I am apprehensive that the officers of this detachment, after our arrival at the Army, will be ordered back to England to join our 2nd Battalion, which is to be quartered in Yorkshire, either at York, Beverley, or Richmond. Yesterday a very fine vessel was burnt in the Tagus. She had been used as a store ship. Our regimental stores were taken out of her a few days ago, but I hear the heavy baggage of three other regiments is entirely destroyed. The last accounts from the Army, our Light troops were advancing, and the 3rd Division had invested Ciudad Rodrigo. The weather is very hot, but I hope our marches to join the Army will be made in the night as much as possible. I am daily expecting to hear from home, and hope you will often write and give me all the news you can. Give my love to my brothers and sisters, and remember me to all enquiring friends.

Your affectionate Son,

R. Knowles, Lt., Royal Fusiliers.

I send this per favour of Mr. Pennie, of our Regiment, who returns to England in consequence of severe wounds.

Postmark, ' Portsmouth, 1 Oc: 1, 1811.'

The Campaign in
The Peninsula

After a delay of one week at Lisbon, the detachments started to join the Army under Lord Wellington. The party of the 7th Royal Fusiliers, in strength nearly equal to half a battalion, was commanded by Lieutenant Charles Barrington, a young officer of three years' service. This is an illustration of the youth of the soldiers who were sent to fill the depleted ranks of Wellington's Army. Another officer, Lieutenant Cameron, who was serving with this draft records in his Journal that 'the men were so young, and were worked so hard, that before the winter was over, 300 had either died or been sent home to England'. The following letter gives the line of march, and, considering the times, and that it was written in a cantonment without any facilities for writing, it is a remarkably good letter.

Aldea de Bisboa, Oct. 7th, 1811.

Dear Father,—I have now the satisfaction of addressing you from a Spanish town, after a long and fatiguing march through Portugal. I wrote you last when on the point of sailing for the river Mondego, where we anchored after three days' passage on the 4th Sept., and immediately landed at Figueras. On the 8th, we commenced our march for the Army. We passed through Monte Mor and Perona to Coimbra, where we arrived on the 11th. On the 14th we proceeded on our march through Algacia, Moita, Galleces, Meneca, Sampayo, Celonio, Bacasal, Castell Boni, Navo de Vene to Fuentes de Quinaldo (the head-quarters of Lord Wellington and also of General Cole, who commands the 4th Division of the Army), where we arrived on the morning of the 25th. At the time our advanced brigade was engaged with the enemy. The Fusilier Brigade had marched about half an hour when we arrived to cover the retreat of the advance, the particulars of which you will see in the Gazette. Our Regiment advanced in line with the 23rd and 48th in close column on each flank, when, having accomplished their object, they gradually returned to their position, where we had the pleasure of joining them.

~

Robert Knowles reached Fuente Guinaldo on 25 September 1811, and it may perhaps be of assistance to the reader if an outline be given of the position of the Army in Portugal, and of the 7th Royal Fusiliers at this time.

On 16 May 1811, the battle of Albuera was won by the British soldier, and not by the Generalship of the Commanders of the allied troops engaged. The hill of Albuera is celebrated in military histories. Imagine six thousand British soldiers fighting for four hours against heavy odds to gain its crest, a heavy rain falling and sometimes obscuring the enemy from their view, and the water-courses of the hillside coloured with blood! Of the 6,000, only 1,500 reached the crest of the hill unwounded. A memorable example of British endurance and pluck.

The 7th Royal Fusiliers and the 23rd Fusiliers formed the Fusilier Brigade of the 4th Division, and in a crisis of the battle these soldiers, under the leadership of Lt.-Colonel Sir William Myers of the 7th, forced their way up the hill, struck and shattered a division of the French in flank, and recaptured six guns. Of those who fought at Albuera it would be invidious to select any Regiment, or section; but, the two Fusilier Regiments were conspicuous. Of the 7th Royal Fusiliers, with the laurels of Albuera fresh upon them, Robert Knowles had now become a member, joining it when it was actually in action, under the immediate direction of the greatest Commander of the day. Lord Wellington was then blockading Ciudad Rodrigo, and his headquarters were at Fuente Guinaldo. For six weeks, he had blockaded the Fortress, and, the garrison being in straits for food, Marshal Marmont resolved to pass in a convoy. With an Army of sixty thousand men, this was not a difficult operation, his adversary not being in a position to fight a general action. Wellington, however, drew in his forces which were scattered in and about El Bodon and Fuente Guinaldo. By so doing, he compelled Marmont to bring up his full strength before the revictualling of the beleaguered Fortress, which was accomplished on 24 September. On the following day, General

Montbrun with fourteen Battalions of Infantry and a strong force of Cavalry advanced on Fuente Guinaldo, and thus began at El Bodon, six miles away, the action which was at its height when Lieutenant Knowles and his detachment arrived at Fuente Guinaldo.

The 3rd Division held the centre of the allied position at El Bodon and Pastores, which were within three miles of Ciudad Rodrigo. The Light Division was on the right at Martiago on the Vadillo river, the 6th Division and a Brigade of Cavalry held the left. The pivot on which they all turned was Fuente Guinaldo, and at that spot was posted the 4th Division with which the 7th Royal Fusiliers were serving.

At daybreak on September 25th, General Montbrun, with fourteen Battalions of Infantry and three Brigades of Cavalry, crossed the Agueda river, and attacked at once our line of Cavalry picquets on the plain in the vicinity of El Bodon. The Frenchmen were met by the 'fighting 3rd' Division under General Sir Thomas Picton. Taken in an exposed and isolated position and with his flank turned, Sir Thomas Picton retired from El Bodon and its vineyards, moving his column slowly across the plain, and, although repeatedly charged by the enemy's Cavalry, and fired at by six guns on his flank and rear, coolly and skilfully withdrew his division. This retreat for six miles was a fine exhibition of nerve and calm self-possession on the part of the Commander, and of steadiness under fire on the part of his officers and men.

When Wellington discovered the object of the French Commander, he sent the 5th Fusiliers, the 77th British, and the 21st Portuguese Regiments, and some Artillery, to occupy the hill over which ran the road to Fuente Guinaldo. The French

Cavalry attacked the hill with great vigour; but, they were again and again driven down the upper slopes. Montbrun brought up his Artillery and soon made an impression, his Cavalry capturing some of our guns. Meanwhile, our Cavalry, by charging too far, became entangled in the vineyards. In this crisis, the 5th Fusiliers performed one of those extraordinary feats of valour which were not infrequent in the campaigns under Wellington. Led by Major Ridge, the 5th Fusiliers dashed at the French Cavalry, and, sending them flying, re-captured the guns. It recalls the rout of the Cavalry at Minden by six British regiments of infantry.

Lord Wellington ordered a general retirement to the plain below, where the 5th and 77th formed one square, and repulsed time after time the Cavalry that charged them. All the forces, being re-united, now retired across the plain to the position at Fuente Guinaldo, which Wellington had defended by entrenchments and three redoubts. It was during this retirement that the Fusilier Brigade—the 7th and 23rd Fusiliers and the 48th Regiment—of the 4th Division came up and covered the withdrawal referred to by Lieutenant Knowles in his letter of October 7th, where he says, when we arrived, 'the Fusilier Brigade had marched about half an hour to cover the retreat of the advance.... Our Regiment advanced in line with the 23rd and 48th in close column on each flank, when, having accomplished their object, they gradually returned to their position, where we had the pleasure of joining them'.

There is one incident in the combat at El Bodon, mentioned by Sir William Napier, which is particularly worthy of note: 'it was in one of the Cavalry encounters that a French officer, in the act of striking at the gallant Felton Harvey of the 14th

Dragoons, perceived that he had only one arm, and with a rapid movement brought down his sword into a salute, and passed on'. Such were the courtesies between gallant men of both nations in this war.

Wellington in remaining at Fuente Guinaldo accepted a great risk which Napier describes as 'above the rules of war'. With a disposable force of 14,000 men and in a moderate position, he confronted 60,000 men, remaining on the spot for thirty-six hours rather than abandon the famous 'Light Division'. That risk was brought about by the deliberate failure of General Robert Craufurd to obey a written order to fall back upon Fuente Guinaldo. General Robert Craufurd, the ablest Lieutenant who ever served under Wellington, was the Commander of the 'Light Division', which was probably the most perfect fighting unit of Wellington's Armies. Receiving the order before 3p.m. he marched only four miles, thus jeopardizing the safety of the whole force. Two Regiments of Picton's Division that were at Pastores, cut off by Montbrun's turning movement, made a march of fifteen hours and reached Fuente Guinaldo at night. Craufurd, without danger, could have done likewise. Wellington took the risk. Craufurd, however, was blind to the offence of disregarding orders from his chief: for, he gave him the simple assurance that he was in no danger. 'But it was through your conduct that there was danger', was the calm and stern reply. Still his fault, Craufurd said to his Staff, referring to his chief, 'he is d——d crusty to-day'.

The letter of 7 October continues, and describes the position at this moment:—

We remained under arms during the night. The Fusiliers formed the left of the line, where it was supposed the enemy would make their principal attack, which was fully expected early in the morning. Lord Wellington remained with us all the night and following day, while the enemy were amusing us by manoeuvring in our front and bringing up their numerous reinforcements. About sunset Lord Wellington left us, and immediately the Army was on the move. Our Regiment brought up the rear of the Division, and marched about eleven o'clock, and did not halt until eleven o'clock the following morning at Aldea de Ponte.

~

At midnight on the 26th, the Army was in retreat, and by a skilful movement, Wellington united the whole twelve miles distant from Fuente Guinaldo, and behind the Villar Mayor.

As the next combat is the first in which Lieutenant Knowles received his baptism of fire, it may be of interest to give the disposition of the various Divisions. The right was held by the 5th Division at Aldea Velha, the 4th and Light Divisions and a Cavalry Brigade were in the centre in front of the village at Alfayates, and behind these, as a reserve, were the 3rd and 7th Divisions. On the left of the latter Division was a convent, whence the line was prolonged by two Portuguese Brigades, the 6th Division and a Cavalry Brigade bringing the line to an end at Bismula.

In the front of the village of Aldea da Ponte, but leaning towards Furcalhous on the right of the position, was a line of our Cavalry picquets. Following in close pursuit, the French came up in force on the morning of the 27th, drove in the

Cavalry picquets, and by ten o'clock were in possession of Aldea da Ponte.

At noon they attacked General Pakenham's Brigade of the Fourth Division, composed of the Fusilier Brigade of the 7th Royal Fusiliers, and the 23rd Fusiliers, and the 48th Regiment, which was posted on a range of heights. Wellington rode up at the critical moment, as he so frequently did, and directed the 7th to charge in line, supporting them on each flank with a Portuguese Regiment in column. Down they went, sending helter-skelter before them, the French, who then, entering a wood, tried to turn the position; but, they were thwarted by our Artillery. Wellington, thereupon, acted on the offensive, and sent the 23rd and a Portuguese Regiment against the left of the French. They were successful, and the village was once more in the possession of the allies. A second party of the enemy coming up joined those who had attacked the village, making a fresh combined attack at five o'clock, and Aldea da Ponte was theirs for the second time. General Pakenham at the head of the two Fusilier Regiments drove them out again; but, as the enemy were in considerable force, and the light failing, and, as he knew that Wellington had fixed upon other ground for fighting a battle, he left Aldea da Ponte and re-occupied his position of the morning.

A description of the fight appears in the letter of 7 October 1811. It is the account of a young enthusiastic officer, fighting with his Regiment, thrilled with all the excitement and glow of a first battle.

The letter of 7 October continues:—

About one o'clock the enemy made their appearance. It was a beautiful sight to see our Cavalry skirmishing with them, but before their superior numbers they gradually retired upon us. Our Light Company, with the Light Companies of the 23rd, 48th, and a Company of Germans, acted in our front. Our Regiment was formed in square to receive their numerous Cavalry, which were rapidly advancing. The 23rd and 48th were also formed in square, a short distance upon our right, and about three thousand Portuguese were formed in line on some rising ground in our rear. Our Cavalry, about 2,000, formed on our left. This was the whole of the force we had to oppose to them on that day. Our Light Infantry gave a good account of the enemy's Cavalry, which retired in confusion. Several columns of Infantry continued to advance rapidly when we were suddenly ordered to form line. The fatigues of the night were forgot when Lord Wellington ordered the Fusiliers to charge the enemy. We advanced steadily against a heavy column of Imperial Guards, but they, perceiving our intention, retired in double quick time. Our Light Infantry poured in a dreadful fire amongst them, and numbers of them lay dead and dying on the field. They attempted to form on a rising ground opposite, where our Artillery did great execution. Our Cavalry and Light Infantry pursued them several miles, and were supported by a Regiment of Portuguese Cacadores. We naturally concluded that we should see no more of them that day, but the rascals had formed a plan to surprise our Light Infantry. About six o'clock we heard our Light Infantry very warmly engaged with them. General Packenham ordered the Fusiliers to fall in, and immediately marched us in the direction of the fire. My Captain was just gone on picket, so that I had the honor of commanding a company in action. We advanced in double quick time, and arrived when they had nearly surrounded the Light Infantry. Our right wing was ordered to charge, and to describe the eagerness of the men to close with them is impossible. General Packenham led us on (he is our Lieut.-Colonel—under such a man cowards would fight). Balls were flying about our ears like a hail-storm. He took off his hat, waved it in the air, and cried out 'Lads! Remember the Fusiliers!'. The huzza that followed intimidated the French, and they ran too fast for our bayonets, but our fire mowed them down by dozens. We pursued them to the skirts of a wood, when we were ordered to retire. Our retiring encouraged the enemy, and the wood appeared like a flame with the fire they opened upon us. We retired in good order, the enemy not knowing the small number of men we had in the field, or they must inevitably have cut us to pieces, as we were afterwards informed by prisoners and deserters that they had eight thousand men in the wood, and the whole of the force we opposed to them did not exceed 500 men. The four companys we charged them with did not exceed 200 men. We had now time to look after our friends. We had four officers wounded, but none of them seriously. Many poor fellows fell on my right and left. One ball grazed my cap, another cut my canteen-strap in two, but I am happy to say there was not one billeted upon my body.

~

During the night, Wellington withdrew his army to a strong position on the Coa, which offered a very narrow frontage for attack. Marmont did not venture to test the strength of his opponent, but contented himself by placing a fresh Garrison in Ciudad Rodrigo. Wellington cantoned his Army along both banks of the Coa, giving them a much-needed rest, at the same time sending the Light Division and a Cavalry Brigade to watch Ciudad Rodrigo.

The letter of 7 October ends, and gives the precise details of the movement of the writer's Regiment:—

On the morning of the 28th the greatest part of our Army was concentrated, but the enemy had received too good a lesson from our Division to follow the whole Army. We remained two nights in a large chestnut grove. We marched on the 1st, 2nd, and arrived at Alameda on the 3rd instant. On the 5th we marched to this place, Aldea de Bisboa. The whole Army, it is supposed, is in winter quarters, as rest is now absolutely necessary to recruit the Army. In the sick returns of last month there was upwards of 22,000 British, and about one-half of the Portuguese Army.

~

The following letter, which is chiefly of a personal and domestic nature, gives the writer's estimation of the Spaniards and the Portuguese:—

To Mr. Robert Knowles.
Aldea de Bisboa, Oct. 8th, 1811.

My dear Father,—I write to you the first opportunity after the marches, counter-marches, and hard fighting we have had. I intended writing immediately after my arrival at the Army, but found it impossible to procure paper. They were all in such a state of confusion, and all our baggage was sent into the rear. I received mine on the 30th in the Chestnut Grove, and to-morrow the first mail for England leaves the Army. I was very unfortunate in my baggage being left behind. All the officers of the detachment were in the same situation; when we received it, it had been pillaged. I had 35 dollars taken out of my port-manteau, besides a quantity of linen. The dollars was the balance due to the company I commanded. I am therefore under the necessity of again calling upon your generosity for the sum of ten pounds to be paid into the hands of Messrs. Greenwood & Co., Army agents, on account of Lieut. H. F. Devey,★ with instructions to them to write to Mr. Devey the day they receive it. He has kindly offered to lend me the sum. Hope you will remit it to Messrs. Greenwood & Co. immediately, and write to me by the same post. I am much disappointed at not hearing from home since I left England, but suppose the reason to be that you are not aware the postage of all letters must be paid in England, which are going abroad. I will now give you a little of the country we passed through. From Figueras to Coimbra is a very fine corn country, and well cultivated. Coimbra is a large town, and has not suffered so much from the French as all the other towns. From Coimbra to Celorico it is a very rocky and mountainous country, but the valleys are full of olive trees, and the mountains covered with vineyards. We marched in the track the French Army retreated. They have destroyed all the villages, and there is scarcely a house with a roof on. The country appears quite de-populated. The little I have seen of the Spaniards I like much better than the Portuguese; they

★ H. Fry Devey, Lieutenant, 30 August 1807.

are a much finer race of people, and take more pains to keep themselves clean. Their land is much better cultivated, and the French have not destroyed any of their villages. I must conclude, begging that you will write immediately on the receipt of this. Please to give my best respects to all my friends, particularly to my Couzin Lomax's; give my best love to my sisters and brothers, and believe me,

Your sincerely affectionate Son,

Robt. Knowles, Lt.,

Royal Fusiliers.

Mr. Devey's address which I wish you to send to:—

Messrs. Greenwood and Co.,

Lieut. H. F. Devey,

7th Fusiliers,

British Army,

Portugal or Spain.

I promised to write to my Couzin John Lomax, ★ but have entirely forgot his address. Please to give it me in your next. If anything particularly interesting occurs I will write home.

P.S.—Lieut. Wray, of our Regiment, desires to be remembered to his brother, who is at Dr. Moor's.

Postmark, 'C 22 OC. 22 1811.'

★ Son of Ellen Knowles who married Richard Lomax, of Harwood, and was a widow in 1779.

A month elapses, when another letter, written to his father, tells of the movements of the Army in a comparatively quiet interlude:—

To Mr. Robert Knowles.
                              Villa de Saya, Nov. 5th, 1811.

Dear Father,—I wrote you last from Aldea de Bisboa on the 8th ult., and on the 12th we were moved to this village, where we remained quiet until Saturday last, when we were suddenly ordered to march in the direction of Quinaldo (you will recollect it is the place I mentioned in my last as having joined our Regiment). We were all of us ignorant of the business we were going upon until we arrived at the end of our march, when we were much mortified to hear that John Bull was too late, and we were ordered to march back to our old quarters on the following day. It was intended that our Division should intercept a large convoy of stores that was going to the relief of Ciudad Rodrigo, escorted by about five thousand men, but the enemy had accomplished their purpose the day before we marched. There has nothing interesting occurred since my last letter. You will see in the papers an account of the capture by the Spaniards of the Governor of Ciudad Rodrigo. He was marched prisoner through this village. The French lately murdered some Spanish prisoners, and they naturally retaliated by murdering some Frenchmen that fell into their hands a few days ago. They have also detected a French spy, and were so kind as to make us a present of a hind quarter, which is hung up a short distance from my billet. A few days ago I visited Almieda. The town is destroyed, and the fortifications are very much injured,

64

but Lord Wellington is now repairing the works. On Sunday I had a very fine view of Ciudad Rodrigo, as I walked within three miles of the town, but hope to have a nearer inspection the ensuing spring. I am sorry to say I have not received a letter from home since I left England, but am daily expecting that pleasure. We have great news from General Hill's Army, but you will see the particulars before we have them, as the only accounts we expect to receive will be through the English papers. On the receipt of the first letter from home I shall again write. Remember me to my sisters, brothers, and all enquiring friends, and believe me,

Your affectionate Son,

R. Knowles, Lieut., R.F.

Postmark, 'Lisbon, De. 13. 1811.'

~

The Governor of Ciudad Rodrigo, to whose capture reference is made, was General Renaud, who had imprudently left a Fortress with a weak escort, and he and his whole party, with 200 head of cattle, were captured by the Spanish Cavalry under Julian Sanchez. The loss of the cattle was of more serious consequence to the Garrison than the loss of the Governor. The position of the Commander was taken by the next senior officer, but, the loss of the cattle could not be made good.

Then, as now, Armies in the field, fighting in an extended area, had less knowledge of what was occurring in other Divisions than had people living at a distance.

General Hill was operating at this time in Estremadura, and his swift and brilliant surprise and dispersion of the force under General Gerard in Arroyo dos Molinos, deservedly established his reputation as a Commander; this is the 'great news' mentioned in the last paragraph but one of the letter of November 5th. In this affair, out of 3,000, only 600 Frenchmen escaped.

In the letter of 3 December 1811, there is no exaggeration of the hardships and privations of the Army at that time. Napier says, 'the pay of the Army was three months in arrears, and the supplies, brought up with difficulty, were very scanty; half and quarter rations were often served, and sometimes the troops were without any bread for three days consecutively.' The labour of preparing for a siege was arduous. It was midwinter and the cantonments were unhealthy from incessant rain. It is not surprising, therefore, that there were 20,000 men in hospital.

To Mr. Robert Knowles.
Barba de Porca, Dec. 3rd, 1811.

My dear Father,—I am happy to acknowledge the receipt of my brother's letter of the 30th Sept. Since I last wrote you on the 4th ult. we have had some very severe marches. On the 11th, four companys of our Regiment marched from Villa de Serva to this village, which is situated upon the Aqueda. Here is the celebrated pass by which the French garrison of Almeida escaped. The river runs rapidly, and the rocks on each side are tremendous. It is really astonishing how they succeeded. On the 23rd, in the morning, we had only ten minutes' notice to march in the direction of Ciudad Rodrigo. We joined our Regiment in the evening at Gallegas, after a march of twenty-five miles. Early in the morning we proceeded on our march to Camp Ello, a miserable village about six miles on the right of Ciudad

Rodrigo. Near this place the enemy must pass if they relieved that fortress. Here we remained until the 29th, when we were ordered to return to our old quarters. The five days we were at Camp Ello we only received one pound of biscuit, and fatigue partys were ordered into the woods to gather acorns as a substitute for bread. In this starving state we had only twenty cottages to quarter seven hundred men. You will agree with me when I say very few men in England would envy our situation. On the 1st instant two officers from each Regiment were ordered to examine the passes over the Aqueda, so as to enable them to conduct the different Regiments in the most expeditious manner to any point that may be required. The enemy's convoys are now at Salamanca, waiting a favourable opportunity of proceeding to the relief of Ciudad Rodrigo, but I believe they will find it a difficult matter unless they collect their immense Army. The deserters from the enemy are very numerous, particularly from Ciudad Rodrigo. The morning we marched to this village we met one officer and twenty-eight men; those from Ciudad Rodrigo say that the garrison is on half allowance. My brother mentions the return of our 2nd Battalion to England, but they are now ordered to Jersey. At present there is no probability of me being ordered to join them. I returned the letters I received from Mr. Wood when at Lisbon, under cover of a letter I wrote you. Chadk. says Mr. James Orrel is anxious to hear from his brother. I mentioned in my last that he is in General Hill's Army in the Alentigo. I am anxiously waiting an answer to my letter of the 8th Oct. I also wrote you on the 4th ult. No doubt you have received both by this time. Our officers and men continue sickly. In our last advance we left nine officers in the rear, but I am thankful my health continues good; better if possible than when in England. We have no news here that is interesting, but are all expecting to advance. I will therefore conclude. Give my best respects to all enquiring friends. Remember me to my sisters and brothers, and believe me,

Your affectionate Son,

Robt. Knowles,
Lieut. Royal Fusiliers.

P.S.—My brother mentions that Startem has been to school to John Lee, but is a great blockhead. I therefore am sorry to hear that he is a favorite with my sister, but I trust he will provide another dog against my return, and send it to same master. You must not forget to remember me to John Lee, and tell him there is plenty of game. One of his dogs would be invaluable if with the Army. A spaniel which he would not harbour was yesterday sold for 100 dollars.

~

The next letter home brings New Year's wishes for 'every pleasure this world can afford'.

Villa de Serva, Dec. 31st, 1811.

Dear Father,—The Army is still in the same quarters, but we are daily expecting a move. It is supposed that Ciudad Rodrigo will be Lord Wellington's first object, as he is making preparations for a siege. Detachments from each Regiment in the 4th Division are employed making gabions and fascines for the erection of batterys, and the battering-train have orders to be in readiness to march at hour's notice. He has also thrown a bridge over the

Aqueda about eight miles from this village and six from Ciudad Rodrigo. The French have detached two Divisions of their Army, and have evacuated Placentia. If we do advance I hope our Regiment will be in the front, as I would prefer fighting to lying in the trenches at this season. The Spaniards annoy the French a great deal in this part of the country. General Mina alone destroyed seven thousand of them the last month. I have not heard from home since the 30th Sept., but suppose your letters must have miscarried. I did not neglect drinking your good health on Christmas Day, nor that of all my absent friends, but must say I envied their situation sitting by a fireside with their bellys full of Christmas pyes, but if they are feasting upon all the luxurys England can afford I shall enjoy them the more when I return, with this satisfaction, that I have fought for my country abroad. While writing the above I received a pressing invitation from Capt. King, of our Regiment, to dine with him and Major Despard. The only news I can give you is that we shall break ground before Ciudad Rodrigo on the 13th inst., for you must know it is now the New Year, and I have the satisfaction to wish you every pleasure this world can afford. If I do not hear from you in answer to a letter of the 8th October in a few days, I shall be under the necessity of drawing a bill upon you for £20. The last letter I wrote you was of the 3rd ult., but have no doubt you have received it by this time. The Army is not so sickly as it was when I last wrote, and it gives me great pleasure to say I remain in perfect health. I will again write you if anything particular occurs. In the meantime, I remain,

Your affectionate Son,

R. Knowles, Lieut., Royal Fusiliers.

Postmark, 'Lisbon, Ja. 22. 1812.'

1812

The New Year was heralded in for the Allied Army by the capture of Ciudad Rodrigo, which Wellington had persistently blockaded.

The foregoing letter tells of making preparation for the siege in connection with which it gives even a date! The 1st, 3rd, 4th, and Light Divisions were selected for this duty, each Division taking its turn in rotation. They had to cross a river, wading sometimes up to the waist, to reach the trenches. The winter was unusually severe, and the Troops suffered great hardships. On 8 January, the Light Division, making a circuit, took up a position distant three miles from the Fortress. In the evening that distinguished soldier, Colonel John Colborne, at the head of two Companies from each of the Regiments of the Light Division, carried by assault the palisaded redoubt Francisco, which was close to the 'Greater Tesson,' the farther of the two ridges on the north side. The operation was well managed by the stormers, whose loss was but trifling, and during the night they made a parallel of 600 yards.

On the 10th, the 4th Division were in the trenches, and opened communications from the parallel to the batteries. By the 19th, the breaches became and, as there was a probability that Marmont might attempt to relieve the fortress, Lord Wellington decided to carry it by assault. His final order showed the confidence which he had in his soldiers. It ended with the imperative command— 'Ciudad Rodrigo must be stormed this evening'. The storming was committed to the 3rd and Light Divisions, and the Portuguese under General Pack. The 4th Division was held in reserve.

The operation was divided into three attacks, right, centre, and left, with a false attack upon the St Jago gate, at the opposite side of the town. The troops in the right attack were to cross the Agueda river, and escalade an outwork in front of the Castle. Colonel O'Toole of the Cacadores was in command. The centre attack was to be made by the 3rd Division, Major Manners commanding the storming-party of five hundred Volunteers, and Major George Napier commanding three hundred men of the Light Division.

All were in their appointed places when the attack was prematurely commenced on the right. The storming parties rushed, with astonishing speed under a heavy fire, into the breaches. The main body of the 3rd Division were the first to get in, and for a short time they drove the French before them; but, they were held up by a tempest of grape and musket-fire, and by the filling-up of the passages with the bodies of the dead and wounded. The stormers of the Light Division jumped into the dark ditch, eleven feet deep, and soon found their way up to the smaller breach, which was so narrow that one gun was sufficient to block it. The officers dashed into it followed by their men, while the supports followed rapidly, and at this point the Fortress was won.

The 43rd enfiladed the defenders, and the explosion of the Magazines at the same time helped the 3rd Division to get in at the centre, the Portuguese on the right gaining also the positions assigned to them. For a short time there was some fighting in the streets; but, soon all was over, and the Governor, who was in the Castle, surrendered his sword to Lieutenant Gurwood, the leader of the 'forlorn hope' of the Light Division.

The French lost 300 killed and 1,500 wounded, while 150 guns with much ammunition were captured. The Allies lost 90 officers and 1,200 men killed and wounded; of these, 60 officers and 650 men were killed, or wounded, at the breaches.

Among the slain were Generals Craufurd and Mackinnon. The former was mortally wounded while directing the attack on the lesser breach, and died a few days afterwards. 'A man of great ability' is his description by one who loved him not. He was a stern disciplinarian and a capable Commander, both liked and feared by the men of the Light Division, whom he had brought as fighting soldiers to the highest point of perfection. In seven minutes the Light Division was packed and under arms ready to march or take its place in a line of battle: and this, not on special occasions, but always. It is the leader-ship that tells, and the 43rd, 52nd, and 95th (now the Rifle Brigade) Regiments were indeed fortunate to have been trained by two Commanders of the eminence of Sir John Moore and General

Robert Craufurd. The personality of Craufurd remained with the Light Division long after he had died. The mortal remains of that intrepid warrior were laid in the breach of the bastion that he had won, and it still bears his name. General Mackinnon was beloved by all who knew him, including Napoleon, with whom, strange to relate, he had been a friend in his youth.

Sir William Napier, who was present with his Regiment, the 43rd, says: 'There died many gallant men, amongst others a Captain of the 45th, of whom it has been felicitously said, that three Generals and seventy other officers had fallen, but the soldiers, fresh from the strife, only talked of Hardyman'.

Many more details are given in the two following letters.

To Mr. Robert Knowles.
Castelheo, Jany. 20th, 1812.

My dear Father,—It gives me great pleasure to inform you that Ciudad Rodrigo has surrendered to our arms. In my last I mentioned the probability of our besieging that fortress. On the 8th instant we marched from our cantonment to St. Felius Chico, near which place we crossed the river Aqueda. The same evening the Light Division took by storm a strong out-work within 400 yards of Ciudad Rodrigo, and broke ground about the same distance from the fortress. On the 9th, the 1st Division relieved the Light; on the 10th we relieved the 1st, and on the 11th the 3rd Division relieved us. The whole duties of the siege have been carried on by the four Divisions I have mentioned. The works were carried on briskly under showers of shot from the enemy, and three battery's were completed, and the guns opened about three o'clock on the evening of the 14th instant. I was on duty in one of the battery's at the time, and consider myself a lucky fellow to escape without a scratch, as my party had the dangerous duty of opening the embrazures for the guns, and the enemy's fire was directed altogether at us. A very fine young man, a lieut. in the Engineers, was mortally wounded when standing by my side. Our guns played their part well, and in one hour silenced all the enemy's guns in their front. Our guns continued to batter in breach until the 19th, when the breach was reported practicable, and the Light Division ordered to assist the Division on duty to storm the place. Our Division was relieved on the 19th by the Third, but the Fusilier Brigade was detained until three o'clock, and we fully expected to share with the Third and Light Divisions the honor of storming the town, and were much annoyed at being ordered into quarters at this village. It is the most painful part of my duty to state the loss it is supposed we have sustained in storming the town, which commenced about seven o'clock in the evening. The 45th and 88th Regts. were the first to enter the breach, and, of course, have suffered the most. It is said we lost about 500 men, including about thirty-five officers. Genl. Crawford is mortally wounded, ★ Col. Coborne, of the

★ The writer was here in error, as Colonel Colborne survived until 1863. Colonel Colborne was for many years known as Sir John Colborne, until he became Field-Marshal Lord Seaton. A distinguished soldier who, upon many occasions, proved himself to be capable of turning the fate of a battle. At Waterloo, though it never received any official recognition, he made the critical and determining attack on the Old Guard. Lord Seaton died in 1863.—L. K.

52nd, killed. Genl. Mackinnon, of the Guards, was killed by the blowing up of a magazine after the town had surrendered; but, you will see the particulars of the siege and the [loss] we have sustained in the Gazette. I believe our Regt. in the whole of the siege has not lost more than fifteen men. We fully expect to march to-morrow, whether to the front or return to our old quarters is uncertain. The garrison of Ciudad Rodrigo are marched as prisoners to Almeada to-day. I am in great haste to be in time for post, therefore must conclude by subscribing myself,

Your affectionate Son,

R. Knowles,
Lieut. R.F.

P.S.—I have not received a letter from home since the 30th Sept., and we have accounts from England up to the 31st Dec. You must be aware, as I mentioned in a former letter, that the postage of all letters from abroad must be paid in England, otherwise they will not be forwarded.

~

In a letter, dated one month later, there are given further details connected with the taking of Ciudad Rodrigo. There were twenty deserters found in the Fortress: some were shot, some were otherwise punished, and some were forgiven:

To Mr. Robert Knowles.

Almada, Feby. 18th, 1812.

Dear Father,—After the lapse of several months I have the
pleasure to acknowledge the receipt of a letter from my brother
of so late a date as the 29th ult. I have wrote you since the fall
of Ciudad Rodrigo, since which time there has nothing particular occurred. We marched a few days ago from Castlejos
through Ciudad Rodrigo to Carpio, and yesterday we came
to this village, but I do not suppose we shall remain here many
days, as it is believed the greatest part of the Army will gradually move to the South, and then we expect to be amused by
the seige of Badajos. We have had a hard day's work, the whole
of our Division having been assembled to see the sentence of a
General Court Martial put in force on two deserters, who were
taken in Ciudad Rodrigo. They were sentenced to be shot; it
was the most awful sight I ever beheld. My brother asks if any
of the Bolton lads are present. I only know one that is with the
Regt., of the name of Robinson. I will make enquirys after the
others, and write you in my next. He also asks after two men
of the name of Jackson; if he will write me when they were
enlisted, and where they come from, I will make enquiry after
them. I was obliged to break off my letter here to perform the
most melancholy part of my duty. I was call'd upon to super-
intend the funeral of a poor fellow in my Company. It would
astonish some of my acquaintances in England to see me acting
in the place of a clergyman, reading the Burial Service, etc.
Our Regt. is still very sickly, and I am sorry to say the mortal-
ity is very great, numbers of our poor fellows dying after three
or four days' sickness. I mentioned in some of my letters that

I should be under the necessity of drawing a bill upon you for £20, but the kindness of a friend has rendered it unnecessary, but hope you will on receipt of this pay into the hands of Messrs. and Co., Army Agents, the sum of £20 to be placed to the account of Lieut. H. F. Devey, of our Regt., and desire the Agents to write him on the receipt of it. I beg you will not lose any time in lodging the money, and be particular in desiring them to write to him without loss of time, as it will be his only receipt for it. I shall anxiously wait an answer to this letter, but in the meantime be so good as to remember me to all enquiring friends, and my best respects to my brothers and sisters.

Your sincerely affectionate Son,

Robt. Knowles, Lieut.,
Fusiliers.

The Third Siege of Badajoz

The third attempt to capture Badajoz, a Spanish town and
fortress on the Portuguese border, began on 15 March 1812,
when Marshal Beresford invested the fortress with the 3rd, 4th,
and Light Divisions, and a Portuguese Brigade, a force in all of
15,000 men. Badajoz was defended by 5,000 French, Hessian,
and Spanish soldiers under a resolute, resourceful French
officer, General Armand Phillipon, who had stored provisions
both for the citizens and for the garrison, sufficient to last three
months: but, he was short of ammunition.

The town stands where a small stream, the Rivillas, runs into
the Guadiano, and the defences consisted of curtains and bastions, from 23 to 30 feet high, with counter-scarps. There was
a castle with numerous outworks, including San Roque, the
Picurina, a redoubt 400 yards from the town, the Pardaleras,

between the Guadiano and Rivillas and 200 yards from the ramparts, but connected therewith and defended by powerful batteries: these were all on the left bank of the Guadiano. On the right bank stood the Fort of San Cristobal, which overlooked the interior of the Castle, and on the western side of it was the redoubt of San Vincente, with three forts, which were mined. The arch of the bridge of San Roque was built up to make an inundation, 18 feet deep. These, briefly, were the main defences.

In the two sieges of 1811, the plan of operations was to assault the castle, at the South-Eastern corner of the fortress, and the redoubt Cristobal. On this occasion, for various reasons, it was decided to attack the bastions of Trinidad and Santa Maria; but, before this could be attempted, the Picurina hill had to be stormed and captured. Preparatory for this, the first communication and parallel were made on 17 March and, one week later, on 25 March, after stupendous difficulties caused by floods and other untoward circumstances, all was ready for the attack. The redoubt was stronger than its appearance indicated; but, in the night of the 25th, General Kempt with 500 men of the 3rd Division carried it by assault, when 319 officers and men were killed or wounded.

Time was running against Wellington. Marshal Soult with an army was approaching him. He sent, therefore, General Graham's Division to take up a position at Albuera to which he purposed withdrawing all but an investing force, and there to offer battle, should the necessity arise. But Wellington's soldiers were fiercely eager for the fray, and, the breaches being considered practicable, an order went forth that the fortress was to be stormed in the night of 6 April. General Picton's Division, 'the fighting 3rd', was to cross the Rivillas stream, and escalade the castle wall, while Major Wilson of the 48th Regiment, with the Guards of the trenches, was to attack San Roque. This was the right attack. In the centre, the 4th and Light Divisions under General Colville and Colonel Barnard were to assault and force the breaches. To the 4th Division was assigned the Trinidad, and to the Light Division the bastion of Santa Maria. Each attack was preceded by forlorn hopes and storming parties of 500 men. The 5th Division while making a feint on Pardaleras were to carry the bastion of San Vincente.

On that dark evening there was but little to show the volcanic forces that lay hidden within the fortress. An occasional light, and the voices of the sentinels on the ramparts passing the report that all was well, gave no indication or hint to the besiegers that the garrison were alert and prepared with every means that the ingenuity of a capable and experienced Commander could devise for the destruction of their assailants. The British longed for the hour when they would be let loose at the Fortress: they were galled by the prolonged restraint, and they hated sieges. The digging and excavating, the long hours in crouching attitudes in wet and muddy trenches, exhausted their patience and irritated them, until their temper was one of suppressed, frenzied, anger. Wellington's order was for a simultaneous attack at 10 o'clock, but a fire-ball or 'carcase', to use the soldiers' term, thrown from the castle disclosed the position and readiness of the 3rd Division, and they were consequently obliged to make an attack, premature by half an hour. The 4th and Light Divisions were compelled to move at the same time, silently and quickly, to the breaches. Major Wilson's detachment consisted of the guards of the trenches, and with these were fifty men of the Royal Fusiliers under Lieutenant Knowles. This was the first party to effect the capture of any portion of the defence, and what happened is best told by Lieutenant Knowles in a letter to his father dated 19 June 1812.

The 3rd Division crossed the Rivillas, but were met with a heavy stream of musketry fire. Rushing forward they placed the scaling ladders against the walls of the castle, and rapidly ascended, only to meet with a terrible fire. The ladders were pushed from the walls, heavy blocks of wood, crushing all beneath, were thrown upon them. They fell back to the shelter of the hill, where they were re-formed. Colonel Ridge of the 5th Fusiliers, in a loud voice called upon his men to follow him, and rushing forward placed a ladder against a lower part of the wall, near an embrasure: another officer, Ensign Canch★, placed a second ladder close to the first: and, in a moment, both officers were on the ramparts, their men crowding after them. The French, astounded by such daring, were driven into the town, and the castle was won, but it was not to be retained if the enemy could prevent it. Bringing up their reserves, they attacked the castle at the main town entrance, but were repulsed, at the cost of the life of that gallant leader, Colonel Ridge, who was shot through the bars of the gate.

Glancing at that part of this terrible fight, where the Light and 4th Divisions were engaged, it is necessary to take the

---

★ Ensign Thomas Canch was not promoted Lieutenant until 1813. He became Adjutant of the 5th Fusiliers in the same year, that position he held until 1830, when he was promoted Captain. Seventeen years a Subaltern! This is an illustration of the injustice that was prevalent in the Army, under the system of promotion by purchase.

main incidents of the struggle of the two Divisions in their proper sequence. The stormers of the Light Division, led the heroic Major O'Hara, rushed forward, jumped into the ditch, and placed their ladders against the walls of the Santa Maria. A bright flashing light, coming as from the earth, illuminated the whole scene, and showed to the defenders who were crowded on the ramparts, the heavy swinging columns of the two British Divisions, following their respective storming-parties. Suddenly, there was a deafening explosion of shell, powder, and powder-barrels, which hurled the storming-parties to atoms. The Light Division were for a moment appalled by the spectacle; but, rending the air with a loud angry shout, they leaped into a ditch. At this moment, the 4th Division came running up, and poured in to the sunken fray. In one place the bottom of the ditch had been scooped out, and filled with water, and into this one hundred men fell and were drowned. They belonged to the two Fusilier Regiments, the 7th and 23rd — the men of Albuera. Those who followed turned to the left and came on the face of the unfinished ravelin. This was mistaken for the breach: but, between the ravelin and the ramparts there was a yawning chasm. Again baffled, there was great confusion as the two Divisions crowded in the ravelin. They made an unexpected rush for the breach, but there across the top glittered a range of sword-blades, keen-edged on both sides, firmly fixed in heavy beams. It was impossible to gain a firm foot-hold, as loose planks studded with nails were laid in the narrow pathway, causing each man who tried to stand on them to fall. The attempt to force an entrance was made again and again. Colonel Macleod of the 43rd was shot in the breach. Two hours of this fruitless carnage convinced the officers and men that they could not get through the breach in the Trinidad, or the Santa Maria. The main attack had failed and 2,000 men had fallen in the effort.

About midnight, Lord Wellington ordered the two Divisions to retire from the breaches, so as to prepare for a second assault. The 3rd Division still held the castle.

General Walker's Brigade of the 5th Division had escaladed the bastion of San Vincente and, fighting their way along the ramparts and into the town, had captured three bastions as they went. The fighting in the town continued for some time, then once more it turned to the ramparts, where its course was checked, and then it turned again back into the town. Finding that the British were momentarily increasing their numbers in the town, the French withdrew from the defence of the breaches, and Badajoz was won, and won, not by the troops of the main attack, but by the 3rd Division which forced its way into the castle—an inspiration of Sir Thomas Picton, who begged that he might be allowed to assault the castle—by Walker's Brigade at San Vincente, and, in some degree, by the guards of the trenches under Wilson.

General Phillipon, who was wounded, surrendered on the following morning.

In this assault, no less than 3,500 British officers and men fell, and, of these, 60 officers and 700 men were killed on the spot. At the breaches the 4th and Light Division each lost 1,200 men, and of the 7th Fusiliers, 5 officers and 44 men were killed, and 13 officers and 121 men were wounded.

This letter, undated, but written on 7 April 1812, the day after the capture of the town of Badajos, gives some vivid personal experiences!

Stamped, 'Packet Letter, Plymouth', and '2/6'.

To Mr. Robert Knowles.

Camp before Badajos.

Dear Father,—It gives me great pleasure to be able to write you after the bloody business on the night of the 6th. At the commencement of the business I had the honourable command of a party of 40 men of our Regt., which, with others of the Division, to the number of 150, under the command of Capt. Horton, of the 23rd, were ordered to storm †[the Raveline], a strong outwork about 100 yards from the town, defended on one side by water and a wall around it about 24 feet in height. After being exposed for half an hour to the hottest fire I was ever under, we succeeded in placing one ladder against the wall, by which my party entered. A Corporal was the first who got into the Fort, and was immediately killed. I was the third man who mounted the ladder. On leaping into the place I was knocked down by a shower of grape which broke my sabre into a hundred pieces. I providentially escaped without any serious injury, although my clothes were torn from my back. My sword hand is much cut and bruised, which accounts

† The words in brackets are almost illegible, probably by reason of the wounded hand.

for my bad writing, and my right side is a little bruised. As I mentioned to you before, my sword was broken in pieces. I therefore picked up my firelock, and with the assistance of eight or ten men who had now got into the Fort, I charged along the ramparts, destroying or disarming all who opposed us. The French Garrison consisted of 150 men, but we only took and destroyed about 60, the remainder made their escape to the town. We found 5 guns in the Fort. After properly securing the Fort, we advanced to assist in the attack of the town. You will see the particulars of the whole business in the Gazette, and as my hand is very painful I must conclude. Suffice it to say our Regt. is cut to pieces; we lost 5 officers kill'd and 12 wounded; our wounded officers will leave the Camp this morning, when there will be only ten officers with the Regt., and scarcely one of them without a bruise. The post will leave the Camp at 10 o'clock, but I will write you by the next. Please to remember me to all enquiring friends, and my best respects for my dear sisters and brothers, and believe me,

Your affectionate Son,

R. Knowles, Lt., Fusiliers.

P.S.—Lieut. Wray, whom my brother has often mentioned, is one of the unfortunate officers who fell in the breach of Badajos.

~

Sir William Napier concludes the narrative of this assault with a splendid testimony:—

'Let any man picture to himself this frightful carnage taking place in a space of less than one hundred square yards. Let him consider that the slain died not all suddenly, nor by one manner of death; that some perished by steel, some by shot, some by water, that some were crushed and mangled by heavy weights, some trampled upon, some dashed to pieces by the fiery explosions; that for hours this destruction was endured without shrinking, and that the town was won at last;—Let any man consider this and he must admit that a British Army bears with it an awful power. Who shall do justice to the bravery of the soldiers? the noble emulation of the officers? who shall measure out the glory of Ridge, of Macleod, of Nicholas, or of O'Hara of the 95th, who perished on the breach at the head of the stormers, and with him nearly all the volunteers of that desperate service. No action, no age ever sent forth braver troops to battle than those who stormed Badajoz'.

O'Hara, when leaving camp for the assault, remarked, 'a Lieutenant-Colonel, or dead-meat, to-morrow'.

The Battle of Salamanca

The Fortress of Ciudad Rodrigo fell in January, and Badajoz in April, and yet the campaign of this year did not begin until June when both armies were assembled for a mighty contest in the open field.

The Royal Fusiliers, with the 4th Division, crossed the Tagus on April 20th, and were quartered at Valongas. The movements of the Regiment and indeed of the Army, is well described in the letter from Salamanca of 19 June 1812, which is a connecting link in the events between the fall of Badajoz, and the movements leading up to the defeat of the French at Salamanca. It gives, moreover, a precise narrative of the part taken by the detachment under the command of Lieutenant Knowles in the storming and capture of San Roque:

To Mr. Robert Knowles.

Camp near Salamanca,
June 19th, 1812.

Dear Father,—I wrote you last on the 7th April, the day after
the storming of Badajos, and promised to write you again by
the next post, but the nature of the wound in my hand rendered
it impossible, although it did not prevent me marching with
my Regt. to the North of Portugal. On our arrival at Valango
I was attacked with a slow fever, from which I barely recovered
when we marched from those quarters on the 5th instant. I was
sent to Celonio, in charge of the sick of the Division, but on
my arrival obtained leave to rejoin my Regt., and by making
a few days forced marches I joined them in camp near Ciudad
Rodrigo on the 12th inst. On the 13th, 14th, 15th, and 16th
we marched toward Salamanca. On the night of the 16th the
enemy evacuated the town, but have left a garrison in two con-
vents which they have fortified. Our battery are in a forward
state, and it is expected will open upon their works to-morrow
morning. The 6th Division and two German Regts. are quartered in the town, and carry on the dutys of the siege. The
Light Division and 3rd Division are in the front of us, about
two miles. Ours and the 5th Division are encamped on the
banks of the Tormes, a most beautiful river which runs close
by the town of Salamanca. The 1st and 7th Divisions are on
our right; they are also encamped on the banks of the river.
I yesterday went over to see the town. The Cathedral surpasses
in grandeur anything I ever saw, and the town excels in every
respect any that I have seen in this country. As soon as we have
taken the enemy's works at Salamanca, it is supposed we shall

advance with the greatest rapidity into the heart of Spain, as it is supposed Marmont cannot collect an Army strong enough to fight us. I mentioned to you in my last that I was not with my Regt. at the storming of Badajos, but on duty in the trenches. Major Wilson, 48th Regt., received orders to attack with 300 men Fort St. Roque (or the Raveline). Our Regt. furnished 50 men for that duty. I apply'd and succeeded in obtaining the command of them. When the 3rd Division commenced their attack upon the Castle we advanced to the Raveline, and after considerable difficulty we succeeded in placing one ladder against the wall, about 24 feet high. A Corporal of mine was the first to mount it, and he was kill'd at the top of it. I was the third or fourth, and when in the act of leaping off the wall into the Fort I was knocked down by a discharge from the enemy, the handle of my sabre broke into a hundred pieces, my hand disabled, and at the same time I received a very severe bruise on my side, and a slight wound, a piece of lead (having penetrated through my haversack, which was nearly filled with bread, meat, and a small stone brandy-bottle for the use of the trenches during the night) lodged upon one side of my ribs, but without doing me any serious injury. I recovered myself as soon as possible, and by the time seven or eight of my brave fellows had got into the Fort, I huzzaed and charged along the ramparts, killing or destroying all who opposed us. I armed myself with the first Frenchman's firelock I met with, and carried it as well as I was able under my arm. The greater part of my party having joined me, we charged into the body of the Fort, when they all cried out 'Prisoners'. I forgot to mention to you the plan of attack: 150 men were to escalade on each side, but by some mistake they all attacked on the contrary side to what I did, and I have the satisfaction to state that my party let them all in at the gates. All the British troops from the trenches were ordered to support the 3rd Division in the Castle, and Major Wilson gave me charge of the Fort, with the remains of my party. From the end of a wall where I seated myself, I had a fine view of the different attacks upon the town. We secured about 60 prisoners, who had concealed themselves in different parts of the Fort, and we kill'd and wounded about twenty-five. My party suffered severely. My sergeant and corporal were kill'd, and about twenty-five men kill'd and wounded.*

~

The forts at Salamanca were captured on 27 June. Seven hundred prisoners, thirty guns, provisions, and a secure passage over the Tormes, were the reward of this success, which was achieved ten days earlier than Marshal Marmont thought possible. Fearing to give his opponent any advantage from a chosen position, Marmont retired, followed by Wellington. On 18 July, the 4th and Light Divisions with a Brigade of Cavalry were engaged all day with several French columns, and the 7th Fusiliers had twenty men wounded. There now occurred one of those instances of strange friendliness between contending Armies which were not infrequent in the Peninsular Campaign. The British Divisions were marching in column, the Light Division being nearest the French, but separated from them by the German Cavalry. Both Armies were moving at a rapid pace for the Guarena river, and the officers on each side, pointing their swords or waving their hands in courtesy, alternated their

* The remainder of this letter is missing.

salutations with loud commands, while they passed from front to rear of their men, to quicken the pace towards the common goal. Such were the civilities the officers of both Armies.

On the morning of 22 July, Marshal Marmont brought more troops within the zone of fire, and occupied a wooded height on which stood an old Chapel. Close by were two hills called the Arapiles, by which name the battle of Salamanca is known to the Spaniards to this day. Wellington seized the farther of the two, while the French occupied the second, and at the same time he sent some companies of the Guards and Royal Fusiliers to drive the enemy out of the village of Arapiles. Wellington, who himself witnessed this action, was so pleased with the manner in which the Fusiliers did their work that he mentioned the name of Captain Crowder in his despatch. The 4th Division was in position on a ridge behind the village, while the 5th and 6th were drawn into the inner slopes of the Arapiles. The 3rd Division under General Pakenham was in a wood near Aides Tejada, where they were hidden from the enemy, while they commanded the main road to Ciudad Rodrigo. The interval between the 3rd and 4th Divisions was occupied by Bradford's Portuguese Brigade, the Spaniards, and the British Cavalry.

Wellington's position was now a strong one, and his hope was that Marmont would attack him. At 2p.m., when at dinner, he received word that the French were moving towards the road to Ciudad Rodrigo. At once, he mounted his horse and earnestly watched the moving columns of the enemy. At 3p.m., when their left was entirely separated from the centre, he said, 'Marmont's good genius has forsaken him 71, and he issued the orders that brought on the battle. The 5th Division formed on the right of the 4th Division, and, with the Portuguese and Cavalry, presented a front to the enemy. The 6th and 7th Divisions, British Cavalry and Spaniards, prolonged the line in the direction of the 3rd Division. When these dispositions were completed, Wellington ordered the 3rd Division, with 12 guns and a Brigade of Cavalry to cross the enemy's line of march. To his brother-in-law, General Pakenham, the Commander of the 3rd Division in Picton's absence, he said, pointing to the column of Thomières, 'Ned, do you see those fellows? Throw your Division into column and drive them to the devil'. The reply was, 'Yes: but, let me grasp that conquering right hand'. As Pakenham's attack developed, the remainder of the first line was ordered to attack. When Marmont saw the 3rd Division break across the path of his column on the Ciudad Rodrigo road, he was dismayed. At 5 o'clock, Pakenham began the battle by falling on the front of the French column as it emerged from a wood, while his guns took it in flank. Disconnected, and with many men still in the wood, it was taken at a great disadvantage, and Pakenham pushed home his success with terrible force. The 4th Division, under General Lowry Cole, deployed into line and, with the 5th, passing the Arapiles village and crossing some heavy ploughed land under a storm of grape, drove General Bonnet's troops back, step by step, to the Southern and Eastern height. The Royal Fusiliers under Major Beatty, in the front line, carried a height and captured 18 guns. The failure of the Portuguese to secure the second of the two Arapiles, left the 7th Fusiliers at the mercy of the French Cavalry and Infantry. Lieutenant Cameron who was present thus describes their position, 'We were at this moment ordered by Major Beatty to retire and form square, a most hazardous movement when the enemy's Infantry were advancing, and within thirty yards of us. The order was only partially heard and obeyed on the right, while on the left we kept up a hot fire on the enemy, who were advancing up-hill, and within a few yards of us. The companies on our right having retired in succession, we found ourselves alone; but, the ground the enemy was ascending was so steep, that we got off without loss. Luckily, while we were forming square to receive Cavalry, the 6th Division came up and received the charge intended for us'.

Marmont and General Bonnet were wounded, Thomières was killed, and though General Bertrand Clausel with wonderful ability restored the battle, the repulse in the first forty minutes, after 5 o'clock, was never really recovered. The fight, however, continued until 10 o'clock, when, under cover of the darkness, Clausel skilfully withdrew, and, from the disordered masses, formed a rear-guard and covered the retreat. The allies lost over 7,000 in killed and wounded; but, the French loss was not less than 12,000, and 7,000 prisoners and eleven guns. The Royal Fusiliers lost one officer and 19 men killed, 10 officers and 170 men wounded.

Thus ended what is considered Wellington's most brilliant battle. The lightning-like stroke when Marmont separated his left from the centre, the screening from the enemy of his own dispositions, his holding back the reserves until the supreme moment, when their appearance seemed to the French to be that of an Army suddenly arising from the ground, are indisputable proofs of good generalship.

This brief outline will help to explain the following letter of Lieutenant Knowles, written three days after the battle, when he was still suffering from the wound in his arm.

To Mr. Robert Knowles.

Salamanca, July 25th, 1812.

Dear Father,—It is with the greatest satisfaction I write you after the glorious victory of the 22nd instant on the heights of Salamanca. The action commenced about four o'clock, by the enemy driving in our Light Infantry, when our Regt. was ordered to their support, and we drove them back in great style. Immediately a general attack commenced. Our Brigade and a Brigade of Portuguese advanced in line against their centre, the enemy keeping an incessant fire upon us from twelve pieces of artillery, but nothing could check our advance, and the enemy retired from the heights they occupied in the greatest confusion. At the same time Genl. Packenham, with the 3rd Division, attacked and turned their left, taking a great number of prisoners, and several pieces of artillery. The enemy again formed upon some heights in front of a large forest, and we commenced a second attack. The enemy, after an obstinate resistance, ran into the woods, great numbers of them throwing away their arms. At the same time the 1st Division turned their right, when the rout became general. Our loss on this memorable day has been very severe:—Genls. Le Marchant and Pack killed, Genls. Beresford, Cotton, Leith, Cole, Clinton, and many other officers of rank wounded. The enemy's loss is estimated at from 10 to 12 thousand men kill'd and wounded, and upwards of four thousand prisoners, with a great number of guns, eagles, and colours. Early in the morning our Army commenced its pursuit, and they have already sent through this town upwards of 4,000 more prisoners. You may calculate upon the destruction of one-half the French Army, as our Army is in full pursuit about 40 miles from this town on the road to Madrid. The French Commissariat have all ran away; they have no bread or meat, and are killing their horses as a substitute. At the conclusion of the action I received a musquet ball in my left arm, but I had it cut out the same night, and I believe the bone is not injured. Our Regt., as usual, has suffered considerably, one capt. killed, one captn. wounded, and nine lieuts. Our Brigade does not exceed 500 men, and they are formed into one Battalion. Our loss fell chiefly upon the 3rd, 4th, 5th, and 6th Divisions. The 1st, 7th, and Light Divisions are in high order, and with the Cavalry are strong enough to fight the enemy if they dare to make a stand. I wrote you last from Camp near this town about the 18th ult. We remained in the neighbourhood covering the operations against the Fort at this town. The enemy lay in our front, and sometimes amused us with a brisk cannonade. The 7th Division had a sharp skirmish, driving the enemy from a hill on our right. On the 26th the enemy retired, and the Fort having surrendered, we pursued them. On the 27th the enemy retired upon ★Toursde Selas, where they crossed the Douro. We remained in Camp on the opposite side the river near Medina del Campo, until the night of the 15th. On the morning of the 18th the enemy came up with us. A heavy cannonade commenced which lasted the whole day. In the evening they came up with us, and their Infantry attempted to turn our left, but were repulsed with great slaughter by the left Brigade of our Division, supported by the Portuguese. Another French column advanced, and we advanced to meet them,

★ Read 'Tordesillas.' Marmont took the direction of the Douro and moved to Tordesillas—Gleig's *Life of Wellington*, p. 167.

but they thought proper to retire in double quick time. On the 20th we again retired. On the 21st we had a great deal of manoeuvring. On the morning of the 22nd there was a sharp skirmish, which lasted about four hours. Lord Wellington did all in his power to entice them upon a hill immediately in our front, which he at last succeeded in doing, and immediately a general attack commenced. Never did a British Army carry on a campaign with so much success, the surprising Genl. Gerard's Corps in the south, the capture of Ciudad Rodrigo, Badajos, [then] at Almarez, and Salamanca, lastly the destruction of one half the French Army has placed our gallant leader amongst the greatest Generals* of modern Europe, and no recompense his country can make him will be too great. I will write you again by the next post, and give you all the news in my power. Please to remember me to my brothers, sisters, and all enquiring friends and believe me,

Your affectionate Son,

R. Knowles, Lt., Fusiliers.

P.S.—Excuse all mistakes and bad writing, as my arm is rather painful, and the post is going.

~

The Royal Fusiliers accompanied Wellington to Madrid and took part in his triumphal entry into the Capital of Spain. It

---

* Note.— In the 'Bible in Spain', by George Borrow, the Spanish curé says that Wellington and General Craufurd dined in his house after the battle. Wellington may have dined there, but Craufurd was lying on the ramparts of Ciudad Rodrigo.

might have been a ceremonial exchange between Governors. At 6 o'clock in the morning of the 12th August, King Joseph with his court left, and at Wellington with his Army marched into Madrid.

Lieutenant Knowles made light of his wound in his home-letters; but, it was officially described as 'severe', and, as he was suffering in addition from fever and ague, he was remaining at Salamanca. The evidence of this is circumstantially precise. It is, moreover, certain that his next letter, bearing the post mark 'Lisbon, September 23rd, 1812,' was written at Salamanca.

Postmark, 'Lisbon. Se. 23, 1812'.

To Mr. Robert Knowles.

Dear Father,—I have been under the necessity of breaking my promise in my letter of the 25th ult., which was to write to you by the next post. I hope you have received it long before this, as it would satisfy you that my wound was of a trifling nature, and I am happy to say that it is now completely healed. Immediately after closing my last letter to you, I was attacked by the ague fever and a most severe bowel complaint, with which I have ever since been confined to my bed, with the exception of four or five days. I trust that I have now banished all my complaints, as I have not had a fit of the ague this last three days, and I am rapidly recovering my strength. I yesterday rode as far as the field of battle, but found myself so very weak that I could not ride over the ground. Our wounded in this town are rapidly recovering, but the officers are extremely ill off, not having a farthing to purchase the comforts which are necessary to men nearly reduced to skeletons by wounds and sickness. The Army is only paid up to the 24th March, but they had the generosity to give to each wounded officer 20 dollars a few days after our arrival in this town. This sum (to a few who nursed it well) has supply'd the necessarys of life; others have sold their horses, asses, or mules; others their epaulettes, watches, rings, etc., and, to the disgrace of John Bull, others have perished for want. These are the sufferings which British wounded officers have been subject to in this town, but thanks to Providence I have not been subject to the least inconvenience. Fortunately I had a few dollars in my possession when I came into the town, which have enabled me to get nearly all a person in my sickly situation could desire. You cannot expect news from me now that I am so far in the rear. The last accounts from the Army they were still in quarters; the 1st, 4th, 5th, and 7th Divns. at the Escurial, the 3rd and Light Divns. at Madrid, the 6th Divn., with the 4th, 5th, 38th, 42nd, and 82nd Regts. were watching the remains of Marmont's Army. Report says that General Maitland has landed at Alicant with an expedition from Sicily. We are anxious to hear what the Russians are doing. I hope they will keep the enemy employed in the north until this country is cleared of them. The Spaniards seem to be actively employed recruiting. The general outcry amongst them is 'Let us have British officers and we will fight like British soldiers'. It is now about thirteen months since I left England, and I have in that time only received three letters from home, the last dated 29th Feby. It is natural to conclude that they could not always miscarry, and therefore that no one writes to me. The subject of Lt. Devey, which I have often wrote about, has given me a great deal of uneasiness. Whether you have lodged the £20 I have so repeatedly mentioned in his hands I am ignorant of. He is now returned to England on account of a wound and bad health. The last communication I had with him he proposed that I should give him your address, and he would write to you for the sum of ten pounds which I have received from him. On his arrival in England, therefore, if you have not lodged the money, I beg you will remit him the sum of ten pounds the first intimation you receive from him, and I also beg that you will pay the postage of all letters to him. I have before stated to you that the Army was six months in arrear of pay, which must be sufficient to show you at once my situation. I have lately been under the necessity of purchasing clothing, etc., to a considerable amount. I am therefore under the most disagreeable but pressing necessity of begging a further remittance of £25, which I request you lodge in my name in the hands of Messrs. Greenwood Co., Army Agents, and desire them to write to me on the receipt of it. By the same post you lodge the money I hope you will write me an account of it. It is extremely painful for me to ask this last remittance; nothing but real want should oblige me to do it. I hope my health will shortly be re-established (it has been very precarious since the seige of Badajos). If it is not, I shall be under the necessity of effecting an exchange into a regt. serving in some other climate. Give my best respects to Mr. Lomax's family, and to all enquiring friends; remember me to my brothers and sisters, and believe me,

Your affectionate Son,

R. Knowles, Lt. Fusiliers.

P.S.—As I do not receive letters from home, it may probably be owing to this circumstance that the postage of all letters for abroad must be paid in England, otherwise they will not be sent.

~

The condition of the wounded who were left at Salamanca was deplorable, and it remains a disgraceful reproach to the British Government of the day. They were without the actual necessities of life, many of them were in want of food, clothing, and medicines. The Army was in arrears of pay, and the Commander-in-chief had not the means for paying the butcher's bill. Many more of the sick and wounded would have died, but for the Commissary-General, Sir James McGrigor, who sent stores authority, and from Madrid on his own responsibility, without authority, and he was censured for so doing.

It is obvious that Lieutenant Knowles, on account of his wound and disease, was unequal for some months to march with his regiment, and to endure the hardships of the campaign. This explains his presence at the Depôt which was established at Santarem on the Tagus, about fifty miles from Lisbon. There is now a gap in the correspondence; for, there is no letter between 23 September 1812 and 7 February 1813, the last of the series, and this is much to be regretted. We can, however, imagine the spectacle of a high-spirited young officer, rejoicing in restoration to health, and chafing at the inaction of an enforced detention at a Depôt, when his regiment is in the field. A staff-appointment, with its daily increase of five shillings to a subaltern's pay, does not lessen his zeal to be with his comrades in the fighting-line, and, in June, he is again with his regiment.

To Mr. Robert Knowles.

Santarem, Feby. 7th, 1813.

Dear Father,—I wrote you last from Lisbon on the 19th Dec., and returned to this on the 24th same month. I was so far recovered that I immediately applied for permission to join my Regt., but was unfortunately detained to do duty in this Depot. About three weeks ago I was ordered to act as Adjutant, and I am still pestered with that troublesome office. From nine o'clock in the morning till six in the evening I have not a spare minute. The constant employment I have had, and the uncertainty of remaining here, has been the cause of my delaying writing to you much longer than I intended. With my new office, I have become a man of business; every post-day I have eight or more letters to answer, and weekly we send in about fifty returns to Hd. Quarters. The Commandant, in direct opposition to my wishes, has reported me to the Adjt. GenI. as a stationary officer at this Depot, so that I can see no prospect of leaving for some time. The last letter I received from home was dated the 17th Nov. The late severe family losses you have sustained distress me excessively, but the miseries I have witnessed and partially endured in this country have in some measure hardened my feelings. It is a subject I cannot dwell upon, therefore will close it. The last mail brought us the most glorious news from Russia; it appears to be almost incredible the success they have obtained over the common enemy. I now feel confident that the business in this country will be decided the ensuing summer, and that I shall soon have the satisfaction of returning to my native land, and conversing about my adventures in the Peninsula.

We have no news at this Depot, therefore must conclude. Remember me to my brothers, sisters, and all enquiring friends, and believe me to remain,

Your affectionate Son,

R. Knowles.

Feby. 9th, 1813.

Our Lt.–Col. Blakeney* passed through this town this morning on his march to the Army. I mentioned my being

* Note.—Lieutenant-Colonel Blakeney became Field-Marshal the Right Honourable Sir Edward Blakeney, G.C.B., G.C.H. He joined the Royal Fusiliers as Major on 24 March 1804, and he was promoted Brevet Lieutenant-Colonel in 1808, and Colonel in 1811. He served with distinction at the capture of Demerara, Berbice, and Essequibo in 1796, and in these operations he had the exceptional experience of being three times taken prisoner by privateers. In 1799, he fought at Egmont-op-Zee and Krabbendem in Holland. He accompanied the expedition to Copenhagen in 1807, and, in 1810, he was again in the West Indies at the capture of Martinique. In that year he went to the Peninsula in command of the 1st Battalion of the Royal Fusiliers, and he was at the head of it in the hard fought battles of Busaco and Albuera, the affair at Aldea da Ponte, the Sieges of Ciudad Rodrigo and Badajoz, the battles of Vittoria, Pyrenees and Nivelle, as well as in various minor actions. He went with the Fusiliers to New Orleans, where he was present at the unfortunate attack on the American lines when General Pakenham was killed. In the Peninsula, he was twice wounded. He served with the Army of occupation in Paris in 1815. He died on 2 August 1868, when he was the Senior Field-Marshal in the Army, and when he had been Governor of the Chelsea Hospital for 12 years.

detained here, and my having been applied to for to accept the Adjutancy of this Depot. He strongly recommended me to join my Regt., but finding that I should not be allowed to do so at present, he advised me to accept the situation of Adjt., saying that, if I must be absent from my regiment, he saw no reason that I should not receive 5s. per day extra, so long as I should be detained. Until I write you the contrary, be so kind as to direct to me at Santarem.

~

In February 1813, the Royal Fusiliers were at Castle Melhor, on the right bank of the Coa, and, towards the end of May, they crossed the Douro and marched to Salamanca. There is no record of the date when Lieutenant Knowles was released from the duties of Adjutant of the Depot, or when he rejoined his regiment; but, it was most probably during May. From 25 May to 19 June, Wellington pursued the French, whose rear-guard he caught on the left bank of the Bayas. With the Light Division he turned the enemy's left flank, attacking them at the same time in front with the 4th Division. The Fusilier Brigade now consisted of the 7th and 23rd Fusiliers, and the 20th and 48th regiments, under Major-General Robert Ross. They all participated in the attack made by the 4th Division. The 7th surprised the French in the village of Montevite, and, with the 20th, followed in pursuit, driving them across the river Zadora. The Fusilier Brigade on the following day held a position on the banks of the Bayas, while the Army was concentrating for a general attack. King Joseph Bonaparte had taken up a position six miles in length and in front of Vittoria, which stands on some rising ground. Wellington's plan of battle was to assail both flanks and, when they had been turned, to send three Divisions against their front. The flank attacks were successful, and the frontal attack was set in motion, when with impetuosity the 3rd Division under Picton broke right through the French centre. With his centre broken and both flanks crushed in, King Joseph had no alternative but to retreat. The last stand was made on some low hills where the fire of eighty guns checked Picton's victorious advance: but, the 4th rushing onwards stormed one hill and forced the French to retire from the others. The Royal Fusiliers took up a position at the bridge of Nanclares. The retreat of the French now became a running-fight for six miles, and, in the confusion and haste, they abandoned guns, baggage, and treasure to the value of one million sterling. There were in some Divisions of the Army excesses; but, in spite of the temptation of rich spoils of war, the discipline of the Royal Fusiliers was such that they marched on, not a man leaving the ranks. On short rations for six weeks, and without food on the 21st, the day of the battle, the men were half starving, and, when they halted at 9 o'clock, they feasted with unbridled indulgence on the sheep, wine and biscuits, which the French had left behind them. The pursuit of the enemy was continued on the 22nd. After a long march, the 7th encamped in the neighbourhood of Pampeluna. On 18 July, the 4th Division marched to the Pyrenees and took up a position in the valley of Urroz, the 7th being two miles in advance at Espinal. On the 24th, they were posted on a mountain to the West of Roncesvalles, in order to secure the pass. Marshal Soult, by whom King Joseph Bonaparte had been superseded, finding the allies were holding a long scattered line, boldly determined to drive them from the Pyrenees.

On the morning of 25 July, he fiercely attacked General Byng's Brigade of the 2nd Division at Roncesvalles. While this combat was proceeding, the Fusilier Brigade advanced under General Ross, up the pass, and at Lindouz they came suddenly upon the head of General Reille's column, which was pushing forward to secure the pass of Atalosti, and thus to cut off Campbell's Portuguese Brigade. Ross could act only on a very narrow front, yet he sent his foremost companies against the French column. This vigorous action secured the pass, and gave General Cole time to concentrate his forces: but, the pass was secured with the loss of many brave soldiers and, among them, was Lieutenant Robert Knowles, the only officer of the 7th Fusiliers who fell on that day. Thus ended, in his twenty-fourth year, the career of this young Englishman. The space of his active military life was two years, but within that short period he had taken part in the two sieges of Ciudad Rodrigo and Badajoz, the action at Aldea da Ponte, and the battles of Salamanca and Vittoria. He suffered bodily-sickness from privations and hardships, and he was wounded twice. At Roncesvalles, he won a soldier's death. There are two qualities which especially appear in the letters, namely, family-affection and the bravery of the soldier. In Japan he would be an ancestor whose spirit would be the object of worship. His life was a fulfilment of the family motto: *nec diu nec frustra* – not for long, and not in vain. His contemporaries, friends, and neighbours, their appreciation of his character and services by erecting to his memory a monument which bears the following inscription:—

Inscription on a Monument in the Parish Church of St Peter, Bolton-le-Moors, Lancashire.

Nec diu nec frustra.

To the Memory of Lieutenant Robert Knowles, a Native of this Parish, who volunteered May 6th, 1811, from the 1st Royal Lancashire Militia into the 7th Regiment of Fusiliers, then united with the British Army in the expulsion of the French from Spain. He distinguished himself at the taking of Ciudad Rodrigo and at Badajos, where he commanded part of a detachment appointed to storm Fort St. Roque. Such was his intrepidity, that having first mounted the wall and succeeded in his enterprise, he opened the Gates to the remainder of the detachment and received the command of the Fort. He behaved with much courage at Salamanca and Vittoria, at the former of which places he was severely wounded. This brave young man fell in the hard-contested Action at the Pass of Roncesvalles, in the Pyrenees, July 25th, 1813, in the 24th year of his age.

This Monument is erected as a just tribute to so much heroism and worth by his Fellow Townsmen, A.D. 1816.

The Knowles Family.

The Knowles family have been long established in Bolton. In the pedigree which appears in Baines's History of the County Palatine and Duchy of Lancaster, edited by James Croston, F.S.A., vo!. 3, page 222, their descent is traced from John Knowle or Knowles, of Edgworth, the son of Richard Knowle or Knowles, who died about the year 1582, and was buried at Bolton. Hereunder is a portion of the pedigree in which-occur the names introduced in the correspondence, together with some later names of members of the family. A very striking feature is the succession of ten members of the Knowles family down to the present day with the alternate names of Robert and Andrew-a long succession, which the Heralds' College think particularly interesting and perhaps unique. A Court Roll of 1651 relating to the Manor of Tottington,

The Knowles family tree from the 1913
edition of Captain Knowles' memoir.

ROBERT KNOWLES,
Of Quarlton. Buried at Turton, 1701.

ANDREW KNOWLES,
Of Quarlton. Buried at Turton, 1730.

ROBERT KNOWLES,
Of Little Bolton. Buried at Turton, 1780.

ANDREW KNOWLES,
Of Quarlton and Eagley Bank, Little Bolton. Buried at Turton, 1810.

ROBERT KNOWLES,
Of Eagley Bank. Buried at Turton, 1819.

CHADWICK,
3rd son.
Buried at Turton,
1817.

ROBERT,
4th son.
Born April 4, 1790.
Killed in action,
July 25, 1813.

JAMES KNOWLES,
6th son.
Town Clerk of Bolton.
Buried at Ainsworth, 1868.

ANDREW KNOWLES,
Of Eagley Bank.
Buried at Turton, 1847.

THOMAS KNOWLES,
Of Cliveley Bank, Clifton.
Buried at Turton, 1872.

JAMES KNOWLES,
Of Eagley Bank.
Buried at Turton, 1886.

ROBERT KNOWLES,
Of Swinton Old Hall.
Buried at Turton, 1883.

ANDREW KNOWLES,
Of Swinton Old Hall.
Buried at Turton, 1890.

ROBERT KNOWLES,
Of Ednaston Lodge, Derby,
High Sheriff of Derbyshire,
1913.
Born 1856.

ANDREW KNOWLES.
Born 1897.

ROBERT MILLINGTON KNOWLES,
Of Colston Bassett Hall, Bingham, Notts,
High Sheriff of Nottinghamshire, 1885-6.
Born 1843.

ANDREW KNOWLES,
Of Newent Court, Gloucester,
High Sheriff of Gloucester-
shire, 1883-4.
Buried at Newent, 1909.

JAMES KNOWLES,
Major, 15th Hussars.
Born 1875.

JOHN KNOWLES,
Of Westwood, Pendlebury,
High Sheriff of Lancashire, 1892-3.
Buried at Pendelbury, 1894.

LEES KNOWLES,
Of Westwood, Pendlebury,
and Turton Tower.
First Baronet.
M.P. West Salford, 1886-1906.
Born 1857.

ARTHUR KNOWLES,
Of Alvaston Hall, Nantwich,
Cheshire,
High Sheriff of Lancashire,
1902-3.
Born 1858.

JOHN BUCHANAN KNOWLES.
Born 1895.

a township contiguous to Quarlton, proves that the Robert Knowles who lived at Quarlton Old Hall, commonly known as Top o' Quarlton, and died in 1701, was of sufficient age to succeed his grandfather, Richard, as heir to the HawkshawEstate, which has descended to the Robert Knowles, of Ednaston Lodge, Derby.

See 'Genealogy of the Knowles Family of Edgworth, Quarlton, Little Bolton, and Swinton,' by the late James C. Scholes, reprinted for private circulation from the ' Bolton Journal ' of 23 January 1886.

General Pakenham

The Honorable Edward Michael Pakenham, second son of the second Baron Longford and brother-in-law of the Duke of Wellington, who had married his sister Catherine in 1806, joined the Army in 1792, and his first commission seems to have been that of Captain in the 92nd Regiment. After serving in several Regiments as Major, he was promoted Lieutenant-Colonel in 1799, and five years later he was transferred to the command of a battalion of the 7th Royal Fusiliers. He was at the head of the 1st Battalion in the expedition to Copenhagen in 1807, and at the capture of Martinique, where he was wounded. In 1809 he was appointed Deputy-Adjutant-General to the Army in the Peninsula. There he subsequently served with marked distinction in command of a Brigade at the battles of Busaco, Fuentes de Onoro, and in many minor actions.

His crowning service was at Salamanca where he commanded the 3rd Division, began the battle, and successfully brought to a triumphant issue Wellington's brilliant stroke. General Pakenham commanded the expedition against New Orleans, where he was killed during the attack on the American lines on 8 January 1815. Thus died Pakenham 'the most frank and gallant of men', in the 36th year of his age, a Major-General and a G.C.B. General Pakenham died unmarried, but the elder branch of his family, the Earls of Longford, have continued the line of distinguished soldiers. His younger brother, Lieutenant-General Sir Hercules R. Pakenham, served with distinction: his eldest son was killed at the Battle of Inkerman, and his third son, Lieutenant-General Thomas Henry Pakenham, C.B., of Longford Lodge, County Antrim, Colonel of the East Lancashire Regiment, died 21 February 1913, aged 86 years. Lieutenant-General Thomas Henry Pakenham, therefore, was a nephew of Major-General Sir Edward Michael Pakenham, who, acting on the command of Wellington, gave the word to his Division and began the movement which won the battle of Salamanca. He entered the Army in 1844, and served in the Crimea, being present at the Battle of the Alma, in which he was twice wounded. His eldest son is Colonel Hercules Arthur Pakenham, commanding the London Irish.

The Duke Of Wellington

Mr. James Knowles, the brother of Lieutenant Robert Knowles, sent the letter of 25 July 1812, describing the battle of Salamanca, written as it was by one who had fought there, to the Duke of Wellington, and in reply he received the following characteristic note. These notes were not uncommon, and they were always in the handwriting of the Duke, who replied, as a rule, without the delay of a day:—

London, May 21st, 1849.

James Knowles, Esq.,
Bolton.

F.M. the Duke of Wellington presents his compliments to Mr. Knowles.

The Duke thanks Mr. Knowles for sending him the letter from his brother written at Salamanca on the 25th July, 1812, giving an account of the Battle of Salamanca, in which he had been present.

He has read the letter with much interest, and returns it.

Extract From Colburn's United Service Magazine, December 1872

'For a few days the Fusiliers were employed in the block-ade of Pampeluna, until the 25th, when they formed part of the force detached to Logrono to intercept General Clausel, who was there with a Division of French who had joined in the battle. Clausel, however, by what Wellington describes as 'some extraordinary forced marches', escaped. The Fusiliers returned to the vicinity of Pampeluna, where they remained a few days, proceeding subsequently to the Pyrenees, the first Division taking post at Viscayret, in the valley of Urroz, the Royal Fusiliers being at Espinal, two miles in advance. On the 2nd July, Soult collected the right and left wings of his army, and on the 25th attacked General Bying's post at Roncesvalles. Lieutenant-General Cole moved up to his support with the First Division. Two companies of the Royal Fusiliers had been advanced on the 24th July to a height westward of Roncesvalles, where they were joined by the remainder of the Battalion during the night, and were consequently ready to meet the French attack. Some sharp fighting occurred during the day, in which the Royal Fusiliers lost Knowles, and six men, killed; one sergeant and 23 men, wounded.'

Addendum

A Letter from the above-mentioned Andrew Orrell.

Andrew Orrell served with his friend Robert Knowles in the Peninsula. He was Ensign in the 34th Regiment, and a letter of this light-hearted soldier speaks for itself:—

Appes. Oct. 4th, 1812.

Yours of the 22nd I received on our march at Quintana. Not having time to answer it before, I now take the opportunity, as we have halted two days. How much longer we shall remain, I cannot say; but, as we are but eight leagues from Madrid, a great party of the officers are gone to visit that city; but, for my part, I shall wait a chance of the Brigade going that way, as our marches have been very considerable. We cross'd the Tagus at Almaraz and marched on for Talavera and Toledo; by the map, you will be able to see our route, as we went by Zafra and Altons and turned to our left, expecting Soult to have gone through La Mancha for Madrid. But the Ape has completely dropt our acquaintance and gone for Valentia with sixty thousand men, and report says that he left that place too; if so, he must have seen his own shadow, as there is no troops to do him much harm: he seems very discontent about things. The people seem all alive here, and strive who can make the most amusement. Last night there was a splendid ball given us, and they requested Brigadier Wilson to give it in orders that they expected all officers to attend; there was a very good turn out of females. We have crost as fine a country as ever was seen, and the town of Toledo is beyond anything I expected to have found; its magnificence is fitting only to be described on a winter's night, when time is not measured. We have abundance of everything, except money: as we have not been paid since April, it is become a scarce thing, but the Spanish Sutlers that accompany the Army, having great confidence in British Officers, supply us on credit with anything we want as teas, sugars, etc. As to pretend to give any particulars as to military affairs is out of the question, but that the French seem to shun us as much as they can. Some people think the game is up, but I think there will be one great struggle. Our confidence is great, and well it may, for our troops are fat, ragged, and saucy; but, never mind! Clothing is coming after us from Lisbon. Wine is abundant in this place, and the inhabitants being free with it, the great difficulty is to keep the men sober. What we shall do next I cannot say, so we must leave it for time to determine. Let me hear from you when this arrives, and often. You mention Mr. Bentley, Captain G. Bambers, etc. When you see them, remember me to them, likewise to Andrew Knowles, ★ and any of the family you may converse with. I hope my Sisters and Brother John are well. I shall conclude with wishing you all every happiness. Remember me to my Uncle and Aunt, etc., etc. W. Bradshaw never wrote to me.—Yours,

A. Orrell,

Ensn. 34th Regt.,
2nd Division British Army, Spain.

(Endorsed) Recd. Novr. 6th, 1812.

~

A description from a endorsement of the service in the Army of Lieutenant Andrew Orrell, who was the younger son of the first Orrell of Meadowcroft Farm, Quarlton.

1803—Sept. 15th.

The service of Lieut. Andrew Orrell, of the 34 Regiment. Then entered Volunteer in the Bolton Volunteer Corps under Lieut.-Colonel Fletcher, being then under 18 years of age, and recd. a Commission for a Lieut. in the Local Militia. Then in the Royal Lancashire Militia.

★ The eldest brother of Lieutenant Robert Knowles, Andrew Knowles, of Eagley Bank, Bolton, was born 16 April 1783, and died 8 December 1847; buried at Turton; will proved at Chester, 27 May 1848.

1811—July 16th. Left Lancashire for the Army.

Then Volunteer'd to the Line and went to Spain. Was in several skirmishes, Left Lancashire was at the affair of Ria de Malina (*sic*), for the Army and got a slight wound in his right hand.

Left Lancashire for the Army.

Was at the Battle of Ronces Valles (*sic*), where he got a severe wound: a ball entered his left breast, and came out within an inch and half of his spine. Remained with the Army till the reduction (Line), and went to Spain.

~

Lieutenant Andrew Orrell was with Lieutenant Knowles in General Hill's Division. He retired on half-pay at the conclusion of the war, lived at Greenthorne, Edgworth, as Colonel Andrew Orrell, and, dying in 1853, he was buried in Turton Churchyard. One of his daughters, Miss Elizabeth Ann Orrell, now resides at 65, Wellington Road, Turton. It may be of interest to mention that Turton Tower was early in the fifteenth century, and until 1628, in the possession of the Orrell family, and that now it has passed to the Knowles family.

A Commission of 1809

The Right Honorable Edward Earl of Derby, Lord Lieutenant of the County Palatine of Lancaster,

To Andrew Orrell, Gentleman.

BY VIRTUE of His Majesty's Commission under His Great Seal of Great Britain constituting me His Lieutenant in and for the County Palatine of Lancaster and in pursuance of the several Statutes in that case made and provided and of the Authorities and powers thereby given and of all other powers and Authorities enabling me thereunto I have presented to His Majesty and HAVE (by and with His Approbation) constituted appointed and given Commission And by these Presents DO constitute appoint and give Commission to you the said

Andrew Orrell to be an Ensign in the First Battalion of the Royal Lancashire Militia forces raised and to be raised for and within the said County Palatine whereof Thomas Stanley Esquire is Colonel pursuant to said Acts. And you are hereby required to train and discipline the persons to be armed and arrayed by Virtue of the several Statutes relating to the Militia forces and in all Things to conform yourself to the Duty of an Ensign of the Militia forces according to the Rules Orders and Directions of the several Acts of Parliament relating thereto and to the true Intent and Meaning thereof GIVEN under my Hand and Seal this thirty-first Day of July in the forty-ninth year of the Reign of our Sovereign Lord George the third and in the year of Lord one thousand eight hundred and nine.

(Signed) DERBY.

A Centenary

Fermoy,

Co. Cork,

July 1st, 1913.

Dear Sir Lees Knowles,—In the name of the 1st Battalion Royal Fusiliers, I beg to thank you most sincerely for your kindness in proposing to dedicate a room in the Union Jack Club for the use of the Royal Fusiliers in memory of your great-great-Uncle. I am sure that this tribute to a gallant Fusilier will be warmly appreciated by all ranks now serving in the Regiment. . . .

I remain,

Yours very truly,

(Signed) R. Fowler-Butler,

Lt.-Col.

Comdg. 1st Battn. Royal Fusiliers.

UNION JACK CLUB,
91a, Waterloo Road, London, S.E.

Room No. 351.

To the Royal Fusiliers,
in Memory of
Lieutenant Robert Knowles,
who fell at Roncesvalles,
July 25th, 1813,
dedicated by his relative,
Sir Lees Knowles, Bar^t, C.V.O.,
July 25th, 1913.

RECOLLECTIONS OF THE STORMING OF THECASTLE OF BADAJOS

Captain MacCarthy

Introduction by Ian Fletcher

Above and following pages: Maps from the 1913 edition of *War in the Peninsula*.

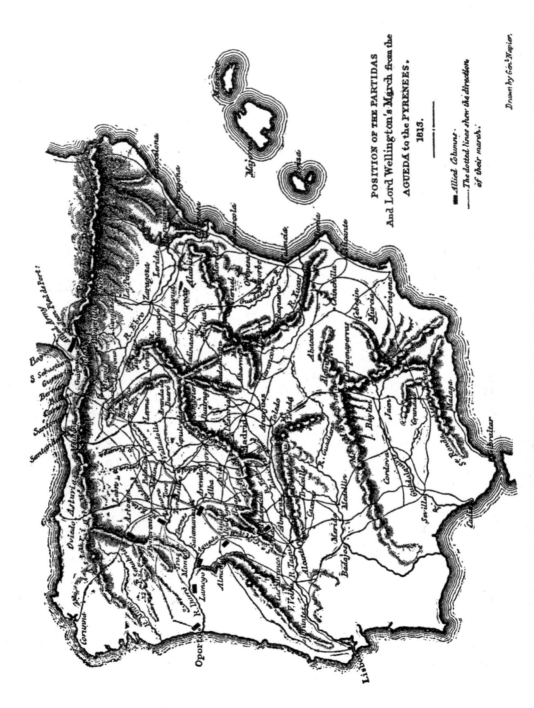

POSITION OF THE PARTIDAS
And Lord Wellington's March from the
AGUEDA to the PYRENEES.
1813.

▬▬▬ Allied Columns.
·········· The dotted lines show the direction
of their march.

Drawn by Col. Napier.

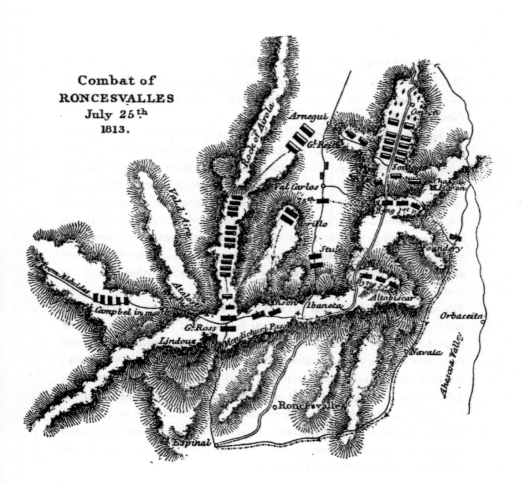

Combat of
RONCESVALLES
July 25th
1813.

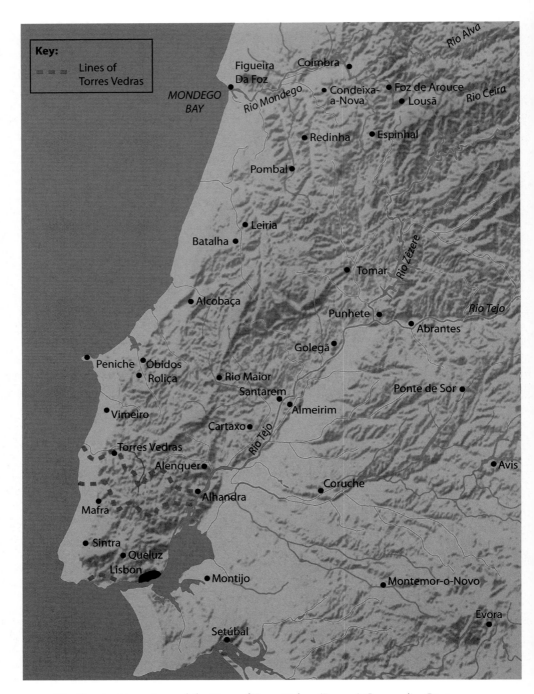

The Vimeiro Campaign and the Lines of Torres Vedras. (From *A Commanding Presence: Wellington in the Peninsula* by Ian Robertson)

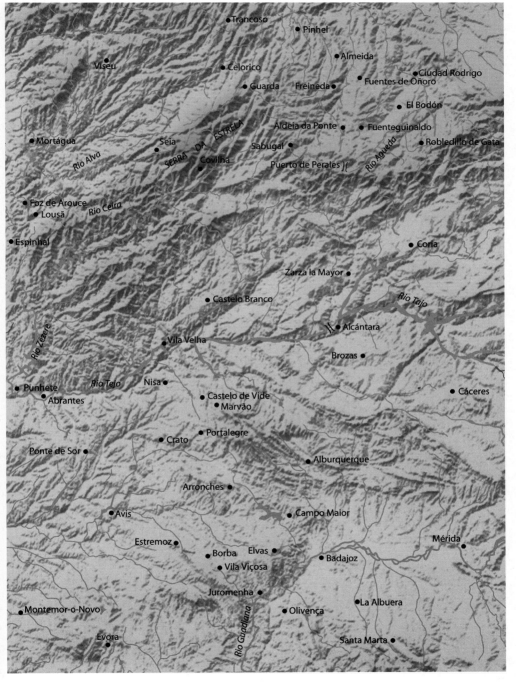

The Ciudad Rordigo–Badajoz corridor; La Albuera. (From *A Commanding Presence: Wellington in the Peninsula* by Ian Robertson)

Adam Neal, 'On the retreat to Corunna'.

A mine exploding during the storming of the main breach at Ciudad Rodrigo.

Thomas St Clair, 'Working parties opening a parallel at Badajoz in June 1811'.

To the MEMORY of
Lieutenant ROBERT KNOWLES, a Native of this
Parish, who volunteered May 6th 1811, from the 1st
Royal Lancashire Militia into the 7th Regiment of
Fusileers, then united with the British Army in the
expulsion of the French from Spain. He distinguished
himself at the taking of Ciudad Rodrigo & at
Badajos where he commanded part of a detachment
appointed to storm Fort St Roque - Such was his
Intrepidity, that having first mounted the Wall &
succeeded in his enterprise he opened the Gates
to the remainder of the detachment and received the
command of the Fort - He behaved with much courage at
Salamanca & Vittoria at the former of which places
he was severely wounded - This brave young Man
fell in the hard contested Action at the pass of
Roncesvalles in the Pyrenees July 25th 1813 in the
24th Year of his Age.
This Monument is erected as a just tribute to so
much Heroism and Worth by his Fellow Townsmen
A.D. 1816.

Memorial erected in Bolton Parish Church to Lieutenant Robert Knowles.

Introduction

The night of 6 April 1812 remains one of the most momentous in the long, bloody and distinguished history of the British Army. After three weeks of toiling in the rain and mud in the trenches in front of the Spanish fortress of Badajoz, Wellington's infantry hurled themselves at the massive walls and despite fierce French resistance that accounted for hundreds of their number, they emerged victorious.

It was a remarkable feat, achieved against the odds, and was one that moved their commander-in-chief, Lord Wellington, never one to eulogise, to pay his men a fine tribute. 'The storming of Badajoz', he wrote, 'affords as strong an instance of the gallantry of the British soldier as has ever been displayed, but I sincerely hope I shall never be the instrument of putting them to such a test as that to which they were put last night.' It was, however, not the first time his men had been asked to fling themselves at the walls of a Spanish fortress, nor would it be the last, but never had so much been asked of them than at Badajoz.

Captain James MacCarthy, of the 50th (West Kent) Regiment – they had yet to be given the Royal prefix – was the assistant engineer attached to Sir Thomas Picton's 3rd Division. His splendid book, *Recollections of the Storming of the Castle of Badajos*, recalls that terrible night when he guided the 3rd Division to the assault, during which he was severely wounded. It is a short but wonderfully descriptive work, full of detail and graphic anecdotes, both horrific and humorous alike. This book, is a reprint of the second edition of MacCarthy's book, originally published in 1836.

The year 1812 had begun in a blaze of glory for Wellington when, on the cold and frosty night of 19 January, his men snatched the Spanish fortress town of Ciudad Rodrigo from the French. Winter was a time when, traditionally, armies went into cantonments to recover from the year's campaigning. But as New Year's Day approached Wellington, the supposed 'cautious general', was planning an audacious attack on the old Moorish town which, if successful, would give him command of the northern corridor between Spain and Portugal.

After just nine days of open trenches Wellington sent in the 3rd and Light Divisions to assault the walls in two places where breaches had been made by the guns of the Royal Artillery. The resistance put up by the French, under General Barrie, was brief and cost the lives of two British major-generals, Robert 'Black Bob' Craufurd and Henry Mackinnon. The Light Division passed relatively easily through the Lesser Breach whilst the 3rd Division successfully stormed the Greater Breach, but not before a huge explosion had sent about 200 of its number hurtling into the sky.

Once inside, the successful stormers dispersed for a brief period while they scoured the houses and shops for drink, food and plunder. Many gathered in the Plaza Mayor and gave vent to their feelings by firing upon the buildings that surrounded it, whilst others set fire to some houses. The period of disorder was brutal, if brief, but the significance of the event should not be overlooked, for it gave the British soldiers a taste of what they could expect and enjoy — if they survived — when they attacked Badajoz, which they knew would be next on Wellington's Spanish wish list.

The capture of Ciudad Rodrigo gave Wellington command of the northern corridor between Spain and Portugal and once this was in his possession he turned his attention to Badajoz, which controlled the southern corridor. The capture of Ciudad Rodrigo came as a great shock to the French, whose winter hibernation had just begun. But if they thought this was the end of Wellington's 'out of season' operations, they were sadly mistaken, for even while his men began repairing the walls of Ciudad Rodrigo, others were slipping away to the south in readiness for the attack on Badajoz

The fortress of Badajoz is a mighty one and is situated on the southern bank of the Guadiana river. Any traffic between Spain and Portugal had to proceed via the town, hence its importance. Any army commander wishing to move either east or west could not even contemplate such a move without possession of the place for if it were left in the hands of the enemy, communications and supply lines would be severely compromised.

When Wellington's men approached Badajoz on 16 March 1812 they did so with the bitter memory of the previous year's failure to take the place etched in their minds. In June 1811, British and Portuguese soldiers had been cut down during two attempts to storm Fort San Christobal, an outwork situated on the northern bank of the Guadiana, possession of which would possibly have forced the French governor of Badajoz, General Armand Phillipon, to surrender the town. But it was not to be. The defenders of Fort San Christobal held out and Wellington was forced to withdraw.

In March 1812 Wellington approached Badajoz with renewed optimism, borne of the success at Ciudad Rodrigo. This optimism was well founded but the siege was far from satisfactory. Indeed, the siege operations in the Peninsula were the most unhappy aspect of what was otherwise a very successful campaign. There was a lack of siege tools, heavy guns were at a premium, and with no trained sappers or miners in Wellington's army, the digging devolved upon the ordinary line infantry who positively loathed the business.

Siege warfare was a science. First of all, engineers had to carry out a thorough reconnaissance of the target in order to identify weak points. When this had been done and the point of attack selected, plans would be drawn up for the construction of trenches, or parallels as they were known, after which batteries were constructed. Then, once the batteries had been armed, the guns would open fire on the selected targets. Even then it was simply a case of blasting away at the walls, for the gunners were trained to fire at the foot of the walls in order to bring the wall tumbling into the ditch. This, in theory, would create a kind of ramp, up which the storming columns would attack. If the breaches were not large enough or if the defences had not been cleared of all obstacles, the consequences for the attacking troops could be dire. Despite the efforts of both engineers and artillery, the siege degenerated into what Wellington later called 'sheer bludgeon work.'

The siege itself was marked by dreadful weather. Heavy rained rendered the effective construction of protective parallels almost impossible. The spoil refused to pile up and instead ran back in streams into the foot of the trench. Wellington's situation was not helped either by the fact that he was up against a resourceful and very active opponent. Indeed, Phillipon was the epitome of an aggressive defender, always encouraging his men, leading sorties and ensuring that the spoil and rubbish which accumulated at the foot of the walls were cleared away each night.

Nevertheless, by the evening of 5 April two large breaches, in the Santa Maria and Trinidad bastions, had been blasted and arrangements made for the assault later that same night. However, whether he was uncertain as to the practicability of the breaches or whether he merely wished to facilitate the path for his stormers, Wellington postponed the attack until a third breach had been made, this time in the curtain wall between the two breached bastions. Throughout the next day, 6 April, Wellington's gunners blasted away at the curtain wall with their huge 24-pounder guns, until by nightfall a third breach had been made. Wellington then issued orders for the attack to take place at nine o'clock that same night.

The attack on the breaches was to be made by the 4th and Light Divisions, with diversionary attacks being made by the 3rd Division, at the Castle, and by the 5th Division, at the San

Vicente bastion, in the north-west corner of the city. These latter two attacks were to be made by escalade, that is to say, with ladders.

Although James MacCarthy was no engineer, he volunteered for service in the engineers' department for the duration of the siege. His own regiment, the 50th, formed part of Rowland Hill's 2nd Division, which played no part in the actual siege. MacCarthy's account of the storming of Badajoz recalls the 3rd Division's attack on the Castle, an attack made by escalade in the face of tremendous French opposition. MacCarthy, in fact, was lucky to get to the Castle, for he was almost cut down by a furious Sir Thomas Picton who, upon hearing the main attacks at the breaches beginning, and sensing that MacCarthy was lost, threatened to cut him down. Ironically, Picton was wounded soon afterwards and thus took no further part in the storming, contrary to numerous contemporary pictures which have him standing on top of the ramparts of the castle.

Initially, few men survived long enough at the top of the walls of the Castle to even shout about it, let alone establish a foothold. The long ladders were filled from top to bottom with eager British soldiers, all of whom were desperate to get inside the city where plunder and pillage awaited them. But the French made them fight for it. With the attack at the breaches floundering in the bloodiest possible style, the success of the two diversionary attacks suddenly became absolutely essential. The British troops stood aghast at the foot of the walls, despairing of ever gaining entry, but, just when all seemed lost, Henry Ridge, of the 5th Foot, gained a foothold on the walls. Another officer followed and suddenly, and miraculously, a group of British soldiers stood defiantly upon the walls of Badajoz.

Others followed and soon hundreds were pouring over into the Castle enclosure. Sadly, Henry Ridge was not among them for he was mortally wounded whilst still on the ramparts.

With the success of the attack by the 3rd Division, Badajoz can be said to have been won. The 5th Division, no less heroic, had achieved its objective and had scaled the walls of the San Vicente bastion. With the two divisions advancing in rear of the French defenders at the breaches, all opposition slacked off and the city was won. The 4th and Light Divisions made over forty separate attacks on the breaches but not one succeeded. Indeed, such were the formidable barriers placed in their way, they were hard pressed to gain entry even in daylight the next morning, and with the French gone.

Some 3,500 casualties were sustained during the assault, mainly at the breaches. It was a savage price to pay, and it is little wonder that Wellington broke down and wept the next morning when he inspected the breaches and saw the shattered remains of two of his finest divisions. Amongst the wounded was MacCarthy himself, which meant that he was not present throughout the following three days of debauchery that followed the storming of Badajoz. Convention of the day dictated that, should a breach be deemed practicable, the garrison would be summoned to surrender and be allowed to march out with honour. Unfortunately, Napoleon decreed that none of his garrison commanders was to surrender a town without first having sustained at least one assault. This, however, meant that the stormers would incur casualties that they considered unnecessary. Thus, in their eyes, the garrison waived all rights to mercy. The strange thing was, that when Wellington's men broke into the town, they took out their anger not on the

French but on the inhabitants of the town and their property. MacCarthy mentions rather quaintly that as a reward for their labours during the siege the men, once inside, would 'rummage the town,' which is putting it mildly. In fact, they were out of control for a full three days before they began to return to their camps.

The sacking of Badajoz was one of the most shameful deeds ever committed by soldiers of the British Army, but who could blame them? Wellington certainly did not. Indeed, one suspects that he felt partly responsible for the catastrophe in the breaches. He later wrote in a letter that had he put the garrison of Ciudad Rodrigo to the sword he would have spared the flower of his army at Badajoz. 'I say this to show that the slaughtering of a garrison is not a useless effusion of blood,' Wellington added chillingly. Unfortunately for the British stormers at Badajoz he spared the garrison of Ciudad Rodrigo and thus the defenders of the former fortress became encouraged to fight on.

Sadly, the harsh lessons of Ciudad Rodrigo and Badajoz were not absorbed by Wellington's army, for the whole process was to be repeated at San Sebastian in 1813, a siege with an equally shocking aftermath. When the town fell on 31 August 1813 it was sacked with a savagery that matched that of Badajoz but was made worse by a fire that engulfed most of the town. Strangely enough, most diarists chose not to go into too much detail, simply writing that the sacking was either as bad, or worse, than at Badajoz. One wonders whether they had simply exhausted themselves in writing of Badajoz and kept the aftermath of San Sebastian short and simple.

Eyewitness accounts of the storming of Badajoz are plentiful enough, as befits the momentous if terrible event. MacCarthy's account, written 24 years later, is one of the rarer ones. The book is not the usual lengthy memoir but is, rather, an account of the siege and storming of Badajoz only, although two pieces at the end of the book recall the storming of Fort Napoleon at Almaraz, in which the 50th played a leading role, and the Battle of Corunna, in which the regiment fought also. It is MacCarthy's account of Badajoz, however, that is the most valuable, not least for the fact that is was MacCarthy who guided the 3rd Division to its attack on the castle. The emphasis is, naturally enough, on the 3rd Division, and on Sir Thomas Picton, for whom MacCarthy obviously had a great deal of admiration, and who died a hero's death at Waterloo in June 1815. Picton's two sisters, in fact, appear on the list of subscribers. Here, then, is MacCarthy's tale of the storming of Badajoz and of his own part in the action, which he modestly describes as being 'only actions of duty.'

Opposite: Title page of the 1836 edition of Captain MacCarthy's memoir.

RECOLLECTIONS

OF

THE STORMING OF THE CASTLE

OF

BADAJOS;

BY THE

THIRD DIVISION, UNDER THE COMMAND OF

LIEUT. GEN. SIR THOMAS PICTON, G.C.B.

ON THE 6th OF APRIL, 1812.

A PERSONAL NARRATIVE,

BY CAPTAIN MAC CARTHY, LATE OF THE 50TH REGIMENT,

ASSISTANT ENGINEER, 3rd DIVISION.

TO WHICH ARE ADDED MEMOIRS OF THE

STORMING OF FORT NAPOLEON, ALMAREZ;

AND OF

THE BATTLE OF CORUNNA.

SECOND EDITION.

LONDON:

PUBLISHED BY W. CLOWES AND SONS, CHARING CROSS.

Address

HAVING been informed by a friend, that he had read 'The Memoirs of Sir Thomas Picton,' in which my name was mentioned; and that a *private* letter of mine to Sir Thomas was inserted in the appendix! I felt considerable regret that I was not apprised, nor aware, of such an intention previously to the appearance of the work, as I might have corresponded — ingenuously — with the author; which, however — besides the inducements herein mentioned—impel me to narrate in the following pages, relative occurrences interesting and authentic—not before published.

Jan. 1st, 1836.

Note

THIS IS not intended as a progressive account of the scientific operations of the Siege of Badajos; nor to publish—vauntingly—my own deeds, which, however arduous, were only actions of duty; but, is designed to supply the vast vacuum in the History of that Siege.

M.

List of Subscribers

His Grace The Duke of Marlborough, (2 copies)
General The Rt. Hon. Lord Hill, G. C. B., G. C. H., K.C.,
Commanding-in-chief
Lt.-General The Rt. Hon. Sir Hussey Vivian, Bart., K.C.B.,
G.C.H. Master-Gen. of the Ordnance
Lt.-General The Hon. Sir Charles Colville, G. C. B. G. C. H.
Lt.-General The Rt. Hon. Lord Howard of Effingham, G.C.B.
Lt.-General The Rt. Hon. Sir George Murray, G.C.B. G. C. H.
Lt.-General The Rt. Hon. Sir James Kempt, G.C.B., G.C.H.
Lt.-General Sir George T. Walker, Bart., G.C.B.
Lt.-General Sir William Hutchinson, K.C.B.
M.-General The Rt. Hon. -Lord Fitz-Roy Somerset, K.C.B.
Col. The Rt. Hon. The Earl of Munster, A.D.C. to the King
The Rt. Hon. Lord John Spencer Churchill

Col. Arnold, K.H., Royal Eng., A.D.C. to the King
Lt.·Colonel Cockburn, Royal Artillery
Lt.-Colonel Thorn, Asst. Q. M. General
Capt. Boxer, R.N., Dover
Major Maling, A. M. Sec. to Com.-in-chief, at the Horse Guards
Major Garvock, Adjutant-general's Office
Captain Roche Meade, K.H., 21st regt. ditto.
Lt.-Colonel Drummond, Heath, Oxford
Captain Stopford, Royal Artillery
Captain Warde, ditto
Lieut. Jephson, (2 copies) ditto
Lieut. Hotham, Royal Engineers
Capt. Dean, 5th regiment Fusiliers
Capt. King, ditto
Ensign Durie, 5th regiment Fusiliers
Ensign Lock, ditto
Ensign Place, ditto
Asst.-Surg. McBean, ditto
T. Robertson, Esq., Oxford
The 50th Regiment N. S. W., (3 copies)
Capt. Serjeantson, 50th regiment, Chatham
Ensign The Hon. E. G. Monkton, ditto, ditto
Asst.-Surg. Graydon, M.D., ditto, ditto
M. Lamert, Esq., late Surgeon, 50th regiment
Lieut. Sawkins, H.P., late of 50th regt.
J. Mac Carthy, Esq., late of 1st (Royal) regiment
Capt. H. Evans, P.B.M.
Capt. Gale, late of 17th regiment
Capt. Rose, 39, Marine Parade, Dover

W. Sprakeling, Esq. H.P., Paymaster Invalid Depôt, Chatham

W. Wyndham, Esq., M. P. The College, Salisbury

W. C. Cotton, Esq., Collector of Customs, Dover

Henshaw Latham, Esq., Dover

Samuel Latham, Esq., ditto

H. Codd, Esq. Kensington

E. Codd, Esq., Fludyer Street

Mr. Court, Dover

H. J. Waddilove, Esq., Lincolns Inn Fields

Lieut. Welsford, 97th regiment

F. Fergusson, Esq., Commander-in-chief's Office

George Collin, Esq., War Office

William Marshall, Esq. ditto

H. Pitman, Esq., Barrack Master, Dover

Lieut. Mac Carthy, 57th regiment

Lieut. Mac Carthy, H. P., 60th Rifles

Captain Marshall, late of 81st regiment

Lt.-Colonel Fulton, 'late 92nd regiment

M.-General The Rt. Hon. Sir H. Hardinge, K. C. B.

Mrs. (Col.) Williams, 'J M St k Sisters of Sir Thos. Picton 1's. o es

Colonel Faunce, C. B.-I.F.O. Bristol, A.D.C. to the King

M.-General The Rt. Hon. Sir H. ,Hardinge, K. C. B.

Mrs. (Col.) Williams & Mrs Stokes — Sisters of Sir Thos. Picton

Colonel Faunce, C. B. —I.F.O. Bristol, A.D.C. to the King

Lt.-Colonel Digby Mackwortl., K. H. -A. D. C. to Lord Hill

Capt. Warde, Royal Artillery, (2nd copy)

Lieut. Massey Dawson, 5th regiment Fusiliers

The Rev. R. B. De Chair, Shepherd's Well

The Rev. Frederick De Chair, East Langdon

Thomas Warner, Esq. Manchester
Mr. R. Page, Dover
Thomas Martin, Esq. M.P. Ballinaherd Castle.

Preface

MANY have written, and many others may write on the same subject, but each in a different theme; because an tell their own story their own way, according to their estimation of the events, on which their conclusions were founded, as exemplified in this narrative; and, there are those, who by compilation assume the character of narrators of what themselves, otherwise, are totally unacquainted with; but the following pages *invite* the recognition of the SURVIVORS of the Siege of Badajos, to FACTS of importance to THEM, interesting to all others, HONOURABLE TO THE BRITISH ARMY, —and, EVERLASTING IN THE PAGE OF HISTORY!

The sublime is truth—and therefore the narrator's pen (like the magnetic-needle) points at accuracy—though he may sometimes have said too little, from intervening circumstances of those NOT within his own observation, where more was required, or expected; and sometimes too much (of himself perhaps) where less would have sufficed. He has also taken the liberty of expressing a few moral reflections on pathetic occurrences, as they arose in his mind.

The continued, unimpaired, and brilliant success of the British arms by sea and land, amidst myriads of obstacles (physical and political) supported by mighty power, is the best proof of the perfection of those establishments! And, on the perusal of the following pages subjects will be found illustrative, unalloyed by flattery or comment; but, creating emulation in the breasts of future warriors—for, men are taught by precedent as well as precept.

The narrator begs to observe, that, in what has been published on the Siege of Badajos, insufficiency is experienced relative to Storming of the Castle, which the following develops and records; and though small in quantity, and concise as is the period this describes, it is hoped that it will be considered extensive in quality: and, notwithstanding it has been admitted that the capture of the Fortress of Badajos was attained by the escalade of its Castle, it is not *fully* known how that event occurred—but the

'MYSTERIOUS KEEPER of the key
—Opes the gate of memory!'

And,

The warrior from strife retired,
By mem'ry his soul's inspired;

And turns to deeds of glory done,
Dangers escap'd, and battles won.

Ruminations and references, therefore, occupied the mind, in selecting interesting occurrences to refresh the narrator's memory—en reverie—in arranging his 'RECOLLECTIONS' of the victorious escalade.

The brilliant conquest of the FORT NAPOLEON; by half a brigade of Lord Hill's Division, so worthy of record, as ONE OF THE GREAT ACHIEVEMENTS OF THE BRITISH ARMY, is little known beyond the official dispatch of the day. But (being confined at Badajos with his wound) at that time, the narrator obtained from brother officers (wounded at Almarez) sojourning with him, and subsequently, from regimental archives and legends, the most interesting particulars, which are here subjoined.

At CORUNNA likewise, (where the narrator was also wounded) the first brigade of General Moore's army, under Lord William Bentinck, sustained the powerful attack of the enemy: this has been only *slightly* noticed in the several publications, occasioned by the difficulty of accurate information being gleaned from the vague reports of the scattered individuals; but, the narrator is enabled of that to add hereto his perfect recollection of that portion of THE BATTLE OF CORUNNA.

Recollections of Storming
The Castle of Badajos

IN presenting to the public biographical illustrations of Lieut. General Sir Thomas Picton, Lieut. General The Right Hon. Sir James Kempt, Major' General The Right Bon. Lord Fitz-Roy Somerset, and others, it is hoped, that possessing several particulars—not made known—which redound to the honour of the gallant Generals, and communicating those FACTS as they occurred in detail, will be acceptable.

The storming of Badajos is an important subject in the page of history: the conquest of the Castle, one of the most arduous and brilliant achievements thereof was accomplished by General Picton's Division—on a plan proposed by himself—; and illumines, forever, his martial fame.

Regard for the memory of General Picton; for the honour and renown of his gallant Division; and, having had the honour—as Assistant-Engineer—of conducting that Division, are inducements to avail myself of this, much-desired, opportunity of explaining my strongly-impressed recollections of that bold and successful enterprise—the escalade of the Castle of Badajos. ——

Lieut. General Sir Thomas Picton's acute ideas, and accurate conception—his presence of mind, and strength of mind, adapted him for enterprize—however perilous; —which, with his martial spirit, always ensured success.

He naturally watched the progress of the Siege of Badajos, and contemplating the means of a termination the most speedy and certain, ran his ideas around the extensive and powerfully defended Fortress, and felt convinced that, as an escalade of the Castle was not likely to be expected by the besieged, THERE was the most accessible point.

Having arranged in his own mind, the escalade, and approaches to the several other objects of attack, and the distribution of the troops, so as to arrest the destructive defences the enemy had prepared against the breaches, and with his reserve to seize the Castle, the General presented those ideas when called upon.

This arduous task was confided to him, and he led his Division to the attack with the utmost confidence: and though wounded early, he had so previously instructed the Brigades, that notwithstanding the enemy on finding the Castle attacked, augmented its defenders and resorted to extraordinary destructives, General Picton's Division prevailed, and exultingly possessed the Castle, enabling the other Divisions of the Army to enter the town.

Thus, it will be shown, was the conquest of the 'Impregnable★ Fortress of Badajos,' attained!!!

I beg the indulgence of refreshing my memory, by commencing with the era of my joining the Besieging-Army, and noting remarkable circumstances during the Siege, to bring perfectly to my remembrance, in detail, the escalade and extraordinary events connected therewith, which fell to the lot of an individual.

To describe the heroism of our soldiers in the Siege, would be impossible; and unnecessary to say more than, that they possessed British hearts: and, of those destined for the escalade of the Castle (within my observations) every individual—officers and men—vied with each other in intrepidity, so devotedly, as to render it difficult to distinguish the BRAVEST *of the* BRAVE!

Being desirous of participating in the Siege of Badajos (on a scale so extensive) and my regiment, in General Hill's Division, then in Albuquerque, I wrote a letter to Colonel Stewart, 50th regiment, soliciting permission to go to the Siege ' on the forlorn-hope duty, should no preferable person be appointed.'—It is said, that who do *only* their duty do WELL; but, that those who volunteer, *do more*.—Three days afterward, my regiment having marched to Merida, general orders were received permitting a portion of officers to serve at the Siege of Badajos as Assistant-Engineers, and requesting their names. I immediately embraced this opportunity, as affording the means of obtaining, by extraordinary exertion, the soldier's reward—approbation and promotion— and sent in my name; as did Captain

★ So named by the French.

Montgomery, who had lately rejoined from the Military College, and was anxious to add practice to theory.

The Division was ordered to Talavera del Real, and Captain Montgomery and myself to proceed forthwith to Badajos.

On entering the encampment on the Talavera side, and enquiring for the Engineers' camp (which was four miles off) we were saluted by many in the regiments we passed through, with the consoling remark (ironically) of, 'here come some more 'Fire-eaters;'' anticipating, I presume, that we were volunteers devoted to the severe duty of Assistant-Engineers.

On arrival late in the day in the Engineers' camp, which was the nighest to the trenches, we reported ourselves to Majors Burgoyne and Squiers (Colonel Fletcher being confined to his pallet by a severe wound): to THEM I expressed my object, and wishes to be employed on extraordinary occasions beyond the usual tour of duty: which I afterwards took an opportunity of repeating to Colonel Fletcher in his tent. I was attached to the 2d Brigade in the charge of Captain——R.E.

The first parallel was commenced, and carried on with great perseverance; and all the batteries which were (temporarily) constructed to protect the working parties, and assail the besieged, were successively dismantled, as the progress of the approaches rendered them unnecessary; previously to which, several of the guns and magazines were injured by the enemy, two or three were dismounted, and in another, a twenty-four-pound shot entered the muzzle of the gun so precisely, as to split it equally on both sides (like the spout of a tea-kettle) as far as the band, and remained there, without disturbing the gun in its position: but, notwithstanding the heavy rains inundated the trenches and decomposed every shovelfull of earth as it was thrown up, so that the embankments could not retain their consistency, the works were continued with extraordinary vigour; and the Engineer department became very severe.

The Engineers were on duty in the trenches eight hours, and off four hours, alternately. The working-parties were relieved every six hours—and the guard in the trenches every twelve hours.

Captain——, R.· E. was a *most singular* character; who, when marking out the ground for No. 7, great breaching battery, very near the wall, which was always lined with French soldiers waiting for objects to fire at, he used to challenge them to prove the perfection of their marksmen, by lifting up the skirts of his coat in defiance, several times in the course of his survey; and then deliberately measuring the ground by prescribed paces, driving stakes, setting spades, &c.; and, when he had finished his task, make his 'congé' by again lifting the skirts of his coat and taking off his hat, amidst their ineffectual firing at him, although a soldier of our working party close to the captain, was stuck, in the act of stooping, by a ball on the pouch-belt where it crosses the bayonet-belt behind. The man screamed with agony, and the French laughed; but on examining him, he was found only to have been hurt by the concussion, both belts and the coat having been cut through as if slit with a penknife, without touching his skin.

Whilst attending the construction of No. 7 battery, I took an opportunity of stepping into Fort Picurina, on the fourth day after the capture of it—the storming of which by 'The Brave General Kempt,' with the 3d Division, was one of the most brilliant exploits of the Peninsular Army. It was a redoubt strongly armed, and surrounded by a deep trench in which were fixed very large earthen-vessels★ filled with combustibles, and furnished above them with bundles of hemp, pitch, &c.; each suspended from the end of a long stake firmly planted in the parapet, and leaned outwards to give light when ignited, and to drip fire into those pots below and cause explosion: the counterscarp was also undermined. This Fort was connected with the Town by a bridge of planks on trestles, over the inundation, the half of which was demolished, and many French soldiers drowned in their panic to regain the Town, and their bodies left floating in the water: several others were left dead in the fosse, but only one British soldier, with green facings. The side of the Fort next the bridge was barricaded with strong palisades, in which was a massive gate, and, being defended by the Fortress, was considered secure; but, so determined and precipitate was the attack, that the enemy had not time to explode the mines. The defence was sanguinary till overpowered by our gallant fellows, and the enemy fled in confusion.—Thus was the capture of Fort Picurina.—I entered by the gate (which was broken) to contemplate the attack and defence, several French soldiers firing at me as soon as I appeared; all was in a state of demolition. A sergeant's guard, consisting of various men of a British Brigade, had charge of the place, and were lolling and laying about; and near them a French soldier laid stretched on his back, his face broiling in the sun. I supposed him dead.—He was without clothes, except a French great coat which was spread upon him. Seeing his right hand upon his face, I approached him—he was alive— and holding his nose with his thumb and fingers. On hearing me speak to the

★ Oil Jars.

sergeant he dropped his hand upon his breast: his mouth was parched and gasping. I took hold of his hand—his pulse seemed regular but strong. I applied to the guard for water,—they had none. I resolved to assist him; but at this moment was recalled to the working men by the arrival of Major Squires, R.E.— involuntarily expressing to the guard my sympathy; and, my regret at the neglect of those whose *duty* it was to adminis- ter assistance in such cases. The guard seemed indifferent to the man. I had not time, then, to ascertain what injuries he had received, and determined to return; which I did in about two hours, and was surprised at not finding the man there. The guard had been relieved, and the new guard knew nothing of the circumstance. I examined the ground, trench, and inunda- tion, supposing him to have expired and been thrown over, or perhaps buried; and made every enquiry but could never gain any information relative to him. This must appear to the reader as extraordinary as to myself—that, a fellow-creature should have remained on the ground in the centre of the Fort severely wounded four days without assistance—or sustenance; and can only be ascribed to the possibility of his having been 'passed by on the other side,' by those who supposed him dead—and I lament, to this moment, that, having found him alive, I had neither 'oil nor wine' to administer unto him.

The day after the above occurrence, a field-officer of the guard in this part, being desirous of examining the town, placed (as was usual) his hat at some distance from himself on the bank, to allure the attention of the French soldiers, who with their muskets presented on their wall, were watching opportunities to fire at individuals. This officer placed his spy- glass on the bank and screened it with a shovel; but, the instant he applied his eye to the glass, a shot from the enemy pierced his forehead, and he fell dead.———Numerous were the accidents and occurrences in the trenches, and some of them very extraordinary.

The enemy kept a guard of several soldiers in the square tower of the church, in Badajos, which had extensive lattices on each side, overlooking the trenches, and by climbing upon the cross-beams, they watched the besiegers, and gave notice when the working parties, or the guard, were being relieved; which, at first, by the reliefs arriving in the works, and the relieved departing, both at the same time, (consisting of between two and three thousand men,) excessively crowded the trenches, among whom the enemy instantly opened a tremendous fire of shot and shell, and caused great destruction. In consequence, the reliefs were ordered not to enter until all those to be relieved had quitted the trenches. Nevertheless, whenever either the working parties or the guard were passing, or any considerable number of men proceeding In the trenches, the enemy, by the information of the watchmen on the church, threw shot and shell with effect. I pointed out to an artillery officer, the fellows in their white trousers, swinging their legs as they sat in the tower, and suggested a shot at them from a twenty-four pounder his men were working, but—'He had no orders.'

The enemy's artillery was directed with great precision. When breaking ground for No. 10 battery we were much annoyed, soon after day-light, by several shots and shells thrown into the work, two of which were remarkable:—The working-party was retiring to make room for the relief, and the last man stood by my side waiting his turn to pass out, (alternately,) and hesitating to allow me to precede him, desired him to pass, as I was not going; at that instant, a cannon shot (lobbed, according to the soldiers' phrase,) fell upon him, and tore out his intestines entire, from his right breast to his left hip, and they hung against his thighs and legs as an apron—instantly he lost his balance and fell. I called a corporal and two men of his regiment to return and bury him, and to report to his commanding officer the circumstance. Having to remain for the succeeding workmen a considerable time before they could arrive, I fixed a shovel in the bank near the same spot, and sat down; and, with two men of the corps of Artificers, were watching the fall of numerous shells thrown at the work, when one of the men said, 'A shell is coming here, Sir.' I looked up, and beheld it approaching me like a cricket-ball to be caught; it travelled so rapidly, that we had only time to run a few paces, and crouch, when it entered the spot on which I had been sitting, and exploding, destroyed all our night's work.

When superintending the opening of the second parallel, about midnight, the enemy, attracted by the sound of the mattocks and spades, directed a constant fire of their musketry upon the working party, and so considerably interrupted the men, that they were obliged to work upon their hands and knees; but, two ingeniously cautious fellows, (taking advantage of the engineer's attention to other parts of the work) dug each a pit of about two yards square, and five feet deep, for themselves to repose in, until routed by the return of the engineer with the field-officer, who, by the bye, finding these 'snug quarters,' took possession, and obliged the men to cut down the partition they had left between the two pits, and continue the trench; (the Portuguese soldiers certainly worked well arid bravely, in competition with the British); during which the attention was attracted by the naked body of a dead man, (a soldier,) about twenty paces distant, which, on examination, appeared to have been buried—hastily—in a very shallow grave, much too short; and, that he had revived and struggled out of it, but expired upon the surface in a writhing position; his body was heaved upwards, supported by his elbows over the sides of the grave, his head bent backwards over one end, and his legs drawn up and resting with his heels over the other end, and quite stiff. He was like a large stool on four legs (viz. head, elbows, and heels) placed over a hole much smaller than itself. A sudden occurrence prevented his being again interred, and he was left to dissolve upon the earth, in the due upon the earth, in the due course of nature, as were numerous brother sufferers in warfare, like all things which have 'run their course,' —men or trees, —and, as an ingredient in the combination of particles for future structures.

No. 7 battery was completed with twelve twenty-four pound-ers; and commenced its tremendous fire about six o'clock in the morning of the 31st of March, which the enemy answered with showers of shot and shells so effectually as to explode the magazine three hours afterwards; and by noon a considerable part of the battery was in ruins. An officer of artillery from this battery met Captain ——*, myself, and two artificers, in the trenches, and told the Captain that he was desired by the officer commanding in No. 7 battery to tell him to inform Colonel Fletcher, that the battery was so much damaged the men could not stand to their guns; and to request that a party might be

*Page 157

sent immediately to repair it. The captain seemed displeased, and replied he could not spare time, and that the artillery officer should carry his message himself. The officer repeated, that he was ordered to deliver this message to the first engineer he met. Captain —— was sent the next day to the Invalid-Depôt at Elvas, on account of an injury he received in his head at the Siege of Rodrigo. I was proceeding afterwards in the trenches, ★ and met two artillery-men carrying, in a blanket, a wounded gunner from this battery, the left side of whose head had been struck by a cannon ball, and his brains, in the unbroken membrane (like a bag) hung on his shoulder. I remonstrated on the uselessness of dragging this poor expiring man to the camp, the half of his head having been shot away. They laid him down to rest themselves and consider, at which moment he expired, and his jaw dropped; and judging that the men had no objection to be employed out of the battery, I recommended them to bury their comrade on the spot, and return immediately to the battery, where they were much required. Soon after, I met some more artillery-men conveying (also in a blanket) from the same battery, an artillery officer, (Capt. Dundas,) very severely wounded, he was a heavy man, and his left arm dreadfully spattered, the shirt and coat torn to rags, his arm was bent and hung over the side, and the weight of his body swagged to the ground. I stopped to assist in putting him in a better position, and laid his left arm straight by his side—his left thigh and leg were also injured. The men proceded with him to the camp. I then passed on to the battery, as a spectator, it was indeed in ruins, the embrasures and buttresses, and nearly all the para-

★On the first, or second day of the operation of No . 7 Battery.

pet, were demolished and open to the town;—it was intensely hot—I remained ten minutes.

The embrasures were repaired, and the bombardment continued vehemently;—the enemy, also, threw some shot and shells in rapid succession.

I proceeded to my duty at the construction of No. 8 breaching battery, where a shell passed over and near me, and sunk into the soft earth of the glacis: having watched it for some time, and remarked to a man by my side, that I thought it would not explode, (I did not then change my position,) immediately it exploded; and, hearing the twirling of a fragment coming toward me, I said to the man, 'here comes a piece of that shell, take care!' —and stepping a short pace to my left, the man did the same—which placed him, unfortunately, nearly in my former position—the fragment passed, and entered deep into the wall of sand-bags near us, when the soldier very calmly said, 'that struck me, Sir;' and, lifting up his right arm, shewed that his hand was torn in strings. He said, 'what shall I do? I replied, 'set off to your camp, to be sure:' and lamented that I had no one to send with him.

Three days before the final assault of Badajos, when employed in converting No. 12 battery, and laying down platforms for ten (I believe) howitzers to cover the advance, all the spare sand-bags were, by desire of Major Burgoyne, to be placed near No. 1 (dismantled) battery, for the convenience of those repairing (from time to time) the breaching batteries. I accompanied the men to shew where to deposit the bags. Two medical officers in blue surtouts and black feathers were here looking into the Town, and invited by the convenience of a scollop in the edge of the bank, had placed their glasses in it. Such scollops were made by round shot from the enemy, but this scollop, I knew from observation, was made, and frequently brushed, by shots from a gun fixed, I supposed, in the Castle, for the purpose of throwing shots into the Engineer-Depot of implements. I passed to lay down the bags a few paces from them, intending to communicate to them their risk, when Lord Wellington, with an officer, came from the breaching batteries, gently walking in the trenches, where shot and shells were flying, as tranquilly as if strolling in his own lawn in England, and on approaching the medical officers, they made their obeisance and offered their glasses, one of which his Lordship politely received, and also placed in the same scollop: at that instant the besieged (perhaps seeing cocked hats) fired the gun, the shot hummed as it passed over Lord Wellington's head, he smiled, but made his inspection, and returned the glass. I paid my respects to his Lordship, 'en passant,' and beheld with astonishment, two private individuals—evidently Londoners—who enquired of me the *shortest* way to the breaching batteries, I consented to escort them, and they walked with me; but prostrating themselves at the report of every gun, remarked that I did not 'duck,' being, they supposed, accustomed to them. On arriving at the end of a new unfinished cut leading from the second parallel direct to the breaching batteries, and near the Town; and being rather waggishly inclined at their request, I informed them this was the *shortest* way, and took leave. I turned back to view them, and beheld both again crouching on 'all-fours,' but laughing heartily. These Londoners, I have reason to believe, were from Mr. Baker's Panorama, in Leicester Square. [Note.—1813. I went on my crutches to view the Panorama of Badajos, where was painted Lord Wellington and the two medical officers, as above mentioned: the artists had not included themselves nor myself, but substituted (for London spectators) a guard in the trenches presenting arms to the Commander-in-chief. And, in the frontispiece of their descriptive pamphlet, was represented, the wounded French soldier in Fort Picurina.] Excuse this digression.

I mentioned in the commencement of these 'Recollections,' that I had expressed a desire of being employed on any extraordinary affair; and therefore received, with great satisfaction, the charge of erecting scaling-ladders:* and Major Burgoyne, with a spyglass, described the mill-dam over which to lead the troops, and the mound (a half sugar-loaf) on the top of which to place five ladders against the wall to reach the parapet, and one ten feet longer against the plane face of the same wall on the right of the mound. —Six ladders were to be reared by Lieut. Cattenagh, 92d regiment, and six ladders by Lieut. —— R.E., but that the ladders on the mound were much relied upon.

With these I was highly gratified, and several times went on a rising ground with a glass to contemplate the point 'd' entrée.' My mind was, in truth, very intent, and anxious for the success of the *task I had solicited.*

The duties in the trenches were conducted by the Hon. Major General Colville, Major General Bowes, and Major General Kempt, under the superintendence of Lieut. General Picton. When General Kempt was on duty in the trenches, his vigilance was proverbial with the soldiers of the working

---

*These were the common sort of ladders, such as are used by builders; and were made of castano (chestnut) trees, in the woods by the men of the staff corps.

parties,—'work away boys, there's one above sees all!'—The Generals were all indefatigable, each remaining on duty twelve hours in the trenches, and were in great danger. General Picton narrowly escaped destruction by a shell which fell upon a man's head in the trench, near No. 3 battery, and exploding at the moment, scattered the man in fragments to the winds.

All the breaching batteries having been completed, directed their vehement bombardment against the bastions of La Trinidad, Santa Maria, and ravelin of Saint Roque; and practical breaches were effected, but rendered inaccessible by the enemy's unusual and formidable entrenchments and defences.

Lieut. General Sir Thomas Graham and Lieut. General Sir R. Hill by their movements obliged the enemy to retire towards Cordova, leaving a small body of cavalry and infantry at Zalamaca de la Serena; and Marshal Soult having quitted Cadiz on the 23rd and 24th of March, marched upon Seville with all the troops, (except about four thousand men,) and proceeding from thence he arrived on the 4th of April at Llerina, and patrolled with strong detachments of cavalry and infantry to Usagre, some leagues nearer Badajos. In the interim General Ballasteros, profitting by Marshal Soult's departure, immediately occupied the place he had left, where his army was received by the inhabitants with the most joyful acclamations. And General Graham, in anticipation, being prepared to retrograde gradually, as was General Hill, from Don Benito and the upper parts of the Guadiana, and to dispose their Divisions in demonstration of resistance to Soult's further advance, completely checked his progress.

The crisis for a grand effort to conquer the Fortress had arrived, and the besiegers were urgent. Several councils were held, and opinions expressed; when General Picton, feeling assured of the inaccessibleness of the breaches—which was afterwards proved correct by the severe losses the 4th and Light Divisions sustained—proposed an escalade of the Castle, and explained his plan, undertaking the performance thereof with his Division; and not meeting with the acquiescence antici-pated, he retired to his camp to await the 'general orders.'

The arrangements in progress were completed, and orders were issued for a general assault at 10 o'clock p.m., assigning to General Picton the escalade of the Castle. The plan was, that Lieut. Gen. Picton should attack the Castle by escalade with the 3rd Division; a detachment from the guard in the trenches of the 4th Division, under the command of Major Wilson, 48th regiment, should attack the ravelin of Saint Roque; the 4th Division, under the Hon. Major General Colville, with the Light Division, under Lieut. Colonel Barnard, to attack the breaches in the bastions of la Trinidad and Santa Maria, and the curtain by which they were connected; the 5th Division, under General Leith, to occupy the ground which the 4th and Light Divisions had occupied during the siege; and Lieut. General Leith to make false attacks upon the outwork Pardileras, and another on the Fort towards the Guadiana, with the left Brigade of the Division under Major-General Walker, which he was to turn into a real attack, if circumstances should prove favorable; Brigadier General Power, with his Portuguese Brigade, to make false attacks on the Tete-du-Pont, the Fort of Saint Christoval, and the new redoubt Mon Creur. By which it appears that the main attacks were the Castle and the breaches; the latter aided by the attack on the ravelin of St. Roque, and all, by the simultaneous false attacks on various points.

The attack of the Fortress was intended on the night of the 5th of April, and myself and others were ordered to attend General Picton in his tent, at eight o'clock in the evening; but the assault was delayed another day, and a breach (3rd) was effected in the curtain of la Trinidad.

To attempt fully to describe the hilarity of the officers and soldiers, individually preparing for a premeditated attack, would be extremely difficult;—the officers with their servants carefully packing their portmanteaus, and the soldiers in like manner packing their knapsacks, to leave in their encampment secure, so as to be readily found on their return, —without, for one moment, considering the certainty of all not returning; the men fixing their best flints in their muskets, and all forming in column, with the utmost alacrity, to march to the assault, deserve the admiration and lasting gratitude of their country. Alas! of all those ardent fellows, many, many never returned.

On the 6th, all minds were anxious for the 'advance,' and orders were issued for the attack at ten o'clock that night. I again, with Major Burgoyne, attended by appointment General Picton, at eight o'clock p.m.: General Kempt and several others were there. General Picton having explained his arrangements and given his orders pulled out his watch, and said, 'It is time, gentlemen, to go:' and added, emphatically, 'Some persons are of opinion that the attack on the Castle will not succeed, but I will forfeit my life if it does not!'

We returned to the Engineer-Depôt, where the fatigue-party and others had assembled to receive ladders, axes, &c., which General Picton superintended himself, and repeated to them some directions. He then asked, 'Who is to show me the way?' and Major Burgoyne presented me to him. When the General had sent off the party, he turned to me, —'Now, sir, I am going to my Division,' —and rode away. I followed and soon lost sight of him in the dark, but pursuing the same direction, (not knowing where the Division was,) I fortunately arrived at the Division, which was drawn up in column between two hills, at the distance, I supposed, of three miles, and quite out of sight of Badajos. General Picton having addressed each of the Brigades, he returned to the head of the Division, ordered the 'march,' and said to me, 'Now, sir, which way are we to go?' We proceeded a considerable distance, and again came within sight of the Fortress; the lights of which were altered and much extended.

I was to conduct to a certain point in the trenches to meet Major Burgoyne, and thence to the escalade; and naturally felt the weight of the charge, when afar in strange ground, where none had before trod; for, if I had misconducted, so that *this* Division arrived too late,★ I cannot, even now, ruminate on the result. But, I had been so perfectly instructed by Major Burgoyne, that I could not err; notwithstanding, to prevent the possibility of deviating, I several times ran ahead to ascertain the correctness of my guidance towards the given point; the General inquiring each time if we were going right, I confidently answered in the affirmative. Again I departed, and approaching in the direction of the ravelin, but far from it, stumbled on a dead soldier of the 52nd regiment, in a spot where I considered he must have been killed in repulsing a sortie of the enemy; which, operating as a landmark, proved that I was perfectly correct. —No delay or error occurred—I

★ Which happened to a distant Division, by the guide mistaking his way.

returned to the column, and informed the General that it was necessary to incline to the right; and, coming to the side of the Talavera road, the column descended into it. Here General Picton, dismounting, sent away his horse, and HEADED HIS DIVISION ON FOOT.

The firing of the enemy's musketry becoming brisk, increased the General's anxiety to be as contiguous as possible, previous to the general assault, lest any occurrence should retard the operation of his Division: and when I had again advanced some distance, to discover Major Burgoyne, and returned, General Picton, emphatically expressing himself, said that I was blind, he supposed, and going wrong; and, drawing his sword, swore he would cut me down. I explained, and he was appeased. I was fully sensible of the high responsibility the General felt for the success of his own proposition of escalading the Castle, (and the more so, as myself solicited the task I had undertaken to perform,) which, added to the prompt decision and intrepidity of character by which General Picton was so eminently distinguished, operated strongly on his mind; and in my own bosom lamented his unnecessary precipitancy, — but I could not repress an involuntary admiration of his ardour! and glanced at the interesting picture of the General, sword-in-hand, and myself before him assuring him of my correctness. We soon after arrived at the very spot, in the first parallel, where Major Burgoyne was waiting; when, seizing his hand, with the affection of a brother-soldier at such a moment, I expressed my happiness on the perfection of my guidance, and my assurance to the General that 'I had not led him an inch out of the way.' Indeed it was as correct as a line.

The Division then entered the trench, and proceeded nearly to the end of it, when the enemy's volcanic fire burst forth in every direction long and far over the Division, and in every kind of combustible. The grandeur of the scene, as Colonel Jones says, was indescribable; but some idea may be formed of its refulgence, by supposing it possible that all the stars, planets, and meteors of the firmament, with innumerable moons emitting smaller ones in their course, were congregated together, and descending upon the heads of the besiegers. Such was the appearance of the fire, raining from the besieged; it was as light as day. —General Picton exclaimed, —'Some of them are too soon; what o'clock is it?' and, comparing his watch with others, the time was a *quarter before ten o'clock*. I mention this, because it has been supposed that General Picton's Division approached too soon. When the Division had advanced some distance from the parallel, and General Picton at its head, with General Kempt, Colonel Burgoyne, the staff, and myself, the enemy's fire increased considerably, and I was walking between General Picton and General Kempt, when General Picton stumbled and dropped wounded in the foot. He was instantly assisted to the left of the column; and the command devolving on General Kempt, he continued to lead it with the greatest gallantry! On arrival at the milldam (extremely narrow), over which the troops were to pass, streams of fire blazed on the Division: the party with ladders, axes, &c., which had preceded, were overwhelmed, mingled in a dense crowd, and stopped the way; being by the side of General Kempt, I said, for recognition sake if we survived, 'This is a glorious night, sir; a glorious night!' and rushing through the crowd, (numbers were sliding into the water and drowning,) I found the ladders left on the palisades in the fosse, and this barrier unbroken; in the exigence, I cried out, 'Down with the paling!' and, aided by the officers and men in rocking the fence, made the opening at which the Division entered; and which being opposite the before-mentioned mound, then, 'Up with the ladders!' —'What! up here?' said a brave officer, (45th). 'Yes!' was replied—and all seizing the ladders, pulled and pushed each other with them up the acclivity of the mound, as the shortest way to its summit. The above officer, and a Major of Brigade, laboriously assisted in raising the ladders against the wall, where the fire was so destructive that with difficulty five ladders were reared on the mound, and I arranged the troops on them successively, according to my instructions, during which I was visited by General Kempt and Major Burgoyne, although this place, and the whole face of the wall, being opposed by the guns of the Citadel, were so swept by their discharges of round-shot, broken shells, bundles of cartridges, and other missiles, and also from the top of the wall, ignited shells, &c., that it was almost impossible to twinkle the eye on any man before he was knocked down. In such an extremity, four of my ladders with troops on them, and an officer on the top of each, were broken, successively, near the upper ends, and slided into the angle of the abutment; —dreadful their fall, and appalling their appearance at day-light. I was forced to the most excessive perseverance of human exertion, and cheered to excite emulation, 'Huzza! they are long enough, push them up again.' On the remaining ladder was no officer; but, a private soldier at the top, in attempting to go over the wall, was shot in the head, as soon as he appeared above the parapet and tumbled backwards to the ground; when the next man [45th regiment] to him upon the ladder instantly sprang over!!! If he was *not* killed, he certainly DESERVED A CROWN OF GLORY in this world; and, if he *was* killed, and brave soldiers are favored IN HEAVEN, HE THERE, NO DOUBT, RECEIVED HIS REWARD! But, so numerous were the INTREPID, that the man above-mentioned could only be distinguished as ONE of the 'BRAVEST OF THE BRAVE'. I instantly cheered 'Huzza, there is one over, follow him!' but the circumstance of the ladders being broken, delayed the escaladers in this part a short time, until the ladders were replaced, so as to reach near the top of the wall, which enabled the troops to pass over; and I frequently cheered, accompanied by the men, to give notice of the successful perseverance of the escaladers to the distant assailants; whose responsive cheers were distinctly heard to be continued around the Fortress.

The 4th and Light Divisions advanced to the assault of the breaches led by their gallant officers, with the utmost intrepidity; but the unusual obstacles prepared by the enemy on the summit, and in rear of the breaches proved so formidable, that our soldiers could not establish themselves; and many brave officers and men, in their perseverance to penetrate, were in succession killed or wounded by explosions on the top of the breaches. The 4th and Light Divisions were, therefore, ordered to retire to the ground they had assembled on immediately previous to the attack: —REMNANTS as they were of those NOBLE DIVISIONS which stood on that ground two short hours before.

The fire of the 4th and Light Divisions, at the breaches, having ceased, enabled the enemy to augment the opposition in these parts, and increase the fire upon the 3rd Division.

About this time General Kempt was wounded: his exertions had been most arduous in bravely visiting, and directing EVERY POINT OF ATTACK, THROUGH THE HEAVIEST FIRE!

After I had arranged the replaced ladders, and in returning to the longest ladder, planted against the wall on the: right of the mound, it was my turn to fall—my right thigh was fractured by a ball which entered the upper part, and fell on a man who had just dropped at my side, with the calf of my leg and heel turned upwards. I instantly seized the trousers, and turned over the limb to preserve existence; and being in a most exposed to the guns, I requested a field-officer★ near to desire some of his men to carry me out of the stream of fire; but (I had occasion to mention him to General Kempt on the mound) he turned himself away, —and one of his men immediately said, 'I'll take you down, sir; can you stand?' —This good fellow took me on his back, but was obliged to drop me, and in a place more exposed. While here, an officer of the 83rd regiment, without his hat, came staggering behind me; and, on approaching, inquired how I was hurt; said he was wounded in the head, and that he would stay by me for mutual consolation, and sat down; but as my spasms were extremely severe, and regular as the pulse, I had no interval for conversation; he left me, and placed himself with his back against the palisades, near the opening, on which the enemy's shots continued to rattle. I saw him in the same position at day-break, but knew not if he was alive or dead. Two other men whom I requested to remove me, were also obliged to set me down—unfortunately—at the base of the mound, with my fractured limb placed upwards on the

★ This officer, I have reason to believe, was killed at Burgos.

bank, so that I could only support myself by placing my hands behind, to prop me in a sitting position; in which I remained immovable till late in the afternoon of the next day, amongst numerous brother sufferers.

The escaladers persevered amidst the determined opposition of the besieged; and the contest at the castle-wall was desperate, the besieged throwing down broken waggons, beams, shot and shells, on the besiegers, and endeavoured to drag the ladders, from the men below.

Lieut. Mc. Alpin, 88th regiment, supposed to have been the first who mounted the castle wall, was there killed. —Several claimed to have been the first up; but, so ardent were all to gain the summit and spring over to the conquest, that it was difficult for the individuals to decide who the first was, as the intrepidity of our troops seemed to have increased in proportion to their difficulties, and to avenge the fall of their Generals, and of their numerous comrades who lay strewed around. It was, indeed, delightful to hear our buglers upon the wall near the citadel, sounding the animating 'ADVANCE,' to proclaim their success, and accelerate the distant troops; which consoled the wounded, and ameliorated their pangs. One bold bugler as soon as he mounted the wall, —determining to be first, — when sounding the 'Advance,' was killed in the act of blasting forth his triumphal music. —The Portuguese Brigade arriving, turned to the right towards the citadel.

Numbers of heroes fell on both sides; —at the castle the bodies of the English and French laid upon each other; — but, General Picton's Division conquered, and was established before twelve o'clock in the citadel,

'The greater part performed, achieve the less!' — DRYDEN

which commanded all the works of the Town, and in the Town; and enabled the other Divisions—which had been powerfully resisted—to enter the Town.

The first person who entered the Town was the gallant Lord Fitz-Roy Somerset, then Secretary to the Commander of the Forces, who, to ascertain the state of the 3rd Division, bravely forced his way through the innumerable obstacles, and imminent dangers of the Town, to the Castle, which he entered, found the 3rd Division established, and reposing in security.

The ravelin of St. Roque was also carried, with the assistance of Major Squires, R.E., by Major Wilson's (48th) detachment of two hundred men, from the guard in the trenches.

Major General Walker advanced with his Brigade, from the barrier on the Olivença road, to make a false attack, entered the covered-way on the left of the bastion of Saint Vincent, and availing himself of the circumstances of the moment, he with great military skill pushed forward, and gallantly escaladed the face of that bastion. Here he was most dangerously wounded.

The 4th and Light Divisions having again formed for the attack, all resistance ceased; and in the morning General Phillipon surrendered, with General Veilande, his staff, and garrison, which he stated consisted of upwards of five thousand men at the commencement, near twelve hundred were killed and wounded, and that about four thousand were prisoners. The garrison, composed of picked men, made a fine appearance when they marched out, after having delivered up their arms. Phillipon had some of the ablest French officers, particularly the Chief Engineer.

General Phillipon finding the Castle wrested from him, had retired, or rather took refuge, in Fort Saint Christoval, and though vanquished, and the whole of the 'Impregnable Fortress' was in the Earl of Wellington's possession, he ostentatiously assumed in the morning a CONSIDERATION of CAPITULATING, until a positive message was repeated, requesting him to attend the Earl of Wellington immediately.

Self-approbation is human nature; and is a predilection all are subject to in various degrees, according as diffidence, or its opposite quality, retract or maintain; and, as all the Divisions exerted their utmost powers to conquer, all (appreciating their own efforts) naturally considered themselves the conquerors; and to them, most justly, is praise due.

Nevertheless, from the foregoing, and In reference to the dispatch of Lord Wellington,★ it will be seen that the conquest of the 'impregnable Fortress of Badajos,' resulted from the escalade and possession of the Castle,—according to General Picton's prediction,—'Some are of opinion that the attack on the Castle will not succeed, but I will forfeit my life if it does not.'

The loss was very considerable; (which General Picton did me the honor of explaining to me in London, ★★ the day before his departure,) would not have happened if his original plan had been wholly executed: and he added many very special circumstances.

† It has been said, 'The plan for attacking Badajos was so extremely hazardous, that, though adopted through necessity,

★ Page 185.

★★ When at breakfast with him, at his lodgings in Baker Street.

from inability to undertake any other, it never was approved of; and Lord Wellington always entertained great doubts of its success.'

† Notwithstanding, so strongly impressed was the mind of General Picton, on the possibility of escalading the Castle, that he pledged his life it would succeed: and so it did, to the dismay of General Phillipon; who, not expecting an attack on the Castle, 'had arranged, in the hope of relief from Soult, to hold the Castle, Tete-du-pont, and Fort Christoval, after the breaches should be forced.★

It has also been asserted that, 'Although General Picton's successful escalade of the Castle placed the garrison at his mercy, yet, the Division remaining therein, produced no other immediate effect, he not having communicated it.'—General Picton had not, it is admitted, the means of communication.

The capture of Badajos, which was the last strong-hold of the enemy on the frontiers of Portugal, animated the Portuguese and Spaniards with the most felicitous anticipations of tranquillity and security; many of the wealthy immediately returned, and engaged in the purchasing of lands, building and repairing dwellings, &c. In Badajos, Elvas, CampoMajor, and in all the Towns I passed through towards Lisbon.

There are few examples in history, of Fortresses of the great strength of Ciudads Rodrigo and Badajos, having been acquired with such rapidity on the part of the besiegers.

† The paragraphs marked and in page 168 accord.
★ Proved by a document found in the Castle.

By these enterprises, and the brilliant capture and destruction of Fort Napoleon,★ Almarez, the enemy felt the 'avengings-word,' and losing all confidence in his own strength, the fertile province of Estremadura became secure from further desolation, and opened, to the allied army and the auxiliary guerillas, Madrid, the Andalusias, Catalonia, and, indeed, the whole of Spain; and obliged the enemy to facilitate the retrograding of his columns, by manoeuvres (always pointing towards home) on fastnesses he had not the power to maintain, and from which his Generals were successively driven.

The encampment was very extensive, some of the Divisions six miles distant from the Fortress:—the Ordnance nearest, and about three miles. Several of the enemy's shot and shells reached the camp; and it was asserted that a shell approached head quarters, and exploded. A Captain of the 42nd regiment, (Monro,) who had arrived in the afternoon of the 6th of April, as a spectator, most gallantly joined the escaladers of the Castle, as a VOLUNTEER, and was killed on the top of a ladder.

An officer I knew, had resolved, on entering the town, to proceed instantly to the church tower, and place his sash upon the flag-staff, above the town colors, in token of victory; but he was severely wounded before an entrance was effected. Many of the soldiers declared during the siege, that, as a compensation for their labor with the pick-axe and spade, they would rummage the town; which they performed for nearly three days; loading themselves with the spoils of bedding, curtains, wearing apparel, plate, &c; and returning to their camp, beating French drums, sounding French bugles, singing, cheering,

★ By the 1st Brigade of General Hill's Division.

and exulting in the most extravagant gesticulations and clam-ors. soldier offered for sale, at my tent, upwards of twenty silver forks, spoons, and solid knife-handles. Many of the Spanish inhabitants were obliged to go into the camp to purchase their *own* clothes of the soldiers.——

I remained where the soldiers were obliged to drop me, at the base of the mound, amidst expiring brother sufferers. During the night, the moans, prayers, cries, and exclamations of the wounded, fully expressed the degrees of their agonies, in the varieties of acuteness and cadence of tone, from the high-est pitch in the treble to the lowest note in bass. Some of the wounded were, undoubtedly, raving mad, violently vociferating dreadful imprecations and denunciations; others singing; and many calling the numbers of their regiments, (as O! 45th.—O! 74th.—O! 77th.) to attract their comrades to their aid. Many of the fallen heroes received additional wounds during the night. One man sat on my left side, rocking to and fro, with his hands across his stomach; in the morning he was dead, stretched on his back, and bleeding out of three wounds in his head, from shots he subsequently received there: his head rested heavily on my hand, which I had not the power to withdraw.

At day-break the wailings of the wounded had been either: silenced by death, or subsided by the exhaustion of the sur-vivors; and the thunder of the guns having ceased on the previous night, was succeeded by a solemnity, which now was more awful to us than the raging of the battle.

The dead and wounded were as close as a regiment laying down to repose;—

'With gasps and glassy eyes they lay,
And reeking limbs immovable.'

and this part becoming the readiest road for the, soldiers—stepping between us—from the Town to the Camp, the cravings
for 'water!' and 'bearers!' were reiterated by all, to those who
approached or passed; but they were too intent on their own
sports, except an artillery-man, who beholding my languor,
kindly administered his blue-bottle (which he had filled with
brandy in the church) to my mouth; the sip revived me, but
I was apprehensive of hemorrhage.—This man promised to
send bearers.★ Late in the afternoon, an officer with bearers
came to take up a man of his regiment, who laid at my side,
with *eleven* shots in him ; and as he was apparently expiring,
and could not be moved, I prevailed on the officer to allow his
men to convey me to my tent; but they were unwilling, and
though obliged to carry me, jostled, and rolled me out of the
bier in going over the mill-dam; they, however, laid me down
on my left side at the end of the second parallel, leaving the
bier † under me, and joined the sports in the Town. I found
myself in a very remote situation, and in danger of remaining

★ I had strictly ordered my servant to seek for me among the fallen, if I did
not return from the attack in the morning; but he had remained in charge
of my baggage, he said;—but I said that he had remained, in preference, in
charge of a large pot of soup and a bag of wine, for regaling himself and
fellow-servant. I dismissed him as soon as another could be obtained.
† A bier is a piece of sacking to lay the wounded soldier upon, with a pole
on each side, and carried by four persons.

undiscovered; in despair, I reached one of the strewed sand-bags, and placing it under my head resigned myself to my fate. Some time afterwards four Spaniards strolled near and examined me, and I requested them to convey me to the camp: they consulted, and refused; but as they were walking off, a surgeon (with buff facings) —most providentially—approached, and seeing me, compelled the fellows to carry me, giving them in charge to a sergeant who was passing, and I arrived at my tent, where surgeon Fitz Patrick, R. A. immediately attended me; then Colonel Robe, R. A. and Majors Burgoyne and Squires visited me, the two latter frequently, and most kindly expressed their approbation of my conduct. On the third day I was removed to the Town; and dreading to be placed in the church among upwards of five hundred on the stone floor, where the difficulty of supplying all their necessities and administering tender care, increased the sufferings of the wounded patients beyond the means in the power of the surgeons to avert, and, in many cases exhaustion and death ensued, which amongst fewer patients might have been ameliorated, I preferred a place alone, and was put into a house pointed out by a surgeon in the street, who recognised me, and expressed his happiness at being able to attend me;—but I did not see him again for three days, when he dropped in for a gossip, without examining or touching my limb. In this manner he, at his leisure, paid me a few visits; and I remained until the middle of May, when my professed friend the doctor called, expressly, as he said, to put me in a proper position, and to set my limb, which had been bent in the fractured part, by the awkward movements, and he desired my servant to call in three or four natives to assist. While the man was gone, the doctor stepped home, 'a few doors;' my servant and the men came, and having waited for the surgeon until they were tired, strolled away—no doctor returned.—But, several hours afterward, I heard him scraping on a violoncello he had previously told me that he found in the church. He called in, on the fourth day, for a moment to tell me that he expected his promotion by the next gazette.——I never more saw him. He was succeeded by a truly worthy man, staff-surgeon Burnal, who immediately had me placed comfortably with my mattress upon the (brick) floor, and set my limb with an eighteen-tail bandage, &c.; he continued to attend me; and also on General Walker,★ and a Lieutenant of the Rifle corps, being three of the worst cases remaining, and which could not be moved when the army departed.

★ General Walker's wound was of a most extraordinarily severe nature—a musket shot cut him across his stomach, grazed the main arteries, which continued oozing for many weeks, hourly threatening hemorrhage; and also detached several ribs from the breast-bone. After a long confinement in Badajos, he was conveyed in his pallet, on men's shoulders, to Lisbon, (a journey of several weeks,) when he embarked for England, and miraculously recovered; and rejoined Lord Wellington's army near Pampeluna, and was again severely wounded.

Extract of A Dispatch from The Earl of Wellington, (Referred To)

Dated, Camp before Badajos, April 7th, 1812.

'THE 4th and Light Divisions having found it impossible to penetrate the obstacles which the enemy had formed to impede their progress,'—attempts were 'repeated till after 12 o'clock at night,'—' and, finding, that success was not likely to be attained; and that General Picton was established in the Castle, I ordered the 4th and Light Divisions to retire.'

'——I have had occasion to mention all these officers [Hon. Major General Colville, Major General Bowes, Major General Kempt, and Lieutenant General Picton,] during the course of the operations; and they all distinguished themselves, and were all wounded in the assault.' The gallantry and conduct of Major General Walker, who was also wounded, and that of the officers and troops under his command, were highly conspicuous.'

'I am particularly obliged to Lieutenant General Picton for the manner in which he arranged the attack of the Castle; and for that in which he supported the attack, and established the troops in that important post.'

'Lieut. General Picton has reported to me, particularly, the conduct of Lieut. Colonel Williams, 60th regiment; Lieut. Colonel Ridge, 5th. regiment, killed in the assault of the Castle; Lieut. Colonel Forbes, 45th regiment; Lieut. Colonel Fitz-Gerald, 60th regiment; Lieut. Colonels Trench and Manners, 74th regiment; Major Carr, 83rd regiment; and the Hon. Major Packenham, Assistant Adjutant General to 3rd Division.'

'He has likewise particularly reported the good conduct of Colonel Campbell, 94th regiment, commanding the Hon. Major General Colville's Brigade during his absence, in command of the 4th Division, whose conduct I have so frequently had occasion to report to your Lordship.'

'The officers and men of the corps of Engineers and Artillery were equally distinguished during the operations of the Siege, and at its close. Lieut. Colonel Fletcher continued to direct the works, (notwithstanding he was wounded in the Sortie, 19th March,) which were carried on by Major Squires, and Major Burgoyne, under his directions. The former established the detachment under Major Wilson in the ravelin of Saint Roque, on the night of the Storm; and the latter attended the attack of the 3rd Division on the Castle.—I have received reports from the General Officers commanding Divisions, of the assistance they received from the officers of those departments attached to them, the greatest number of whom, and all their personal staff, are wounded.'

General Picton has been severely and unjustly censured, in several publications, &c. by those whose minds generated disappointment in proportion to the estimation on which their expectations were founded,—for not having, as was alleged, recommended heroic officers under his command at Rodrigo and Badajos; which he has declared, that was a duty he never neglected, and, in many instances, frequently repeated; and therefore having done his utmost, blame did not attach to him—for instance, 'Ever since that time (Badajos) I have made repeated applications in favor of my own Aide-de-camp, who was most severely wounded there, without success; although I consider his promotion, in consequence, due to me as much as my daily pay-nor can I account for the omission. '—This declaration of his own feelings—made to myself—and expressed in most benign accents, without a breath of allusion to any person, or complaint, must for ever silence any suspicion of General Picton's neglect; and refutes the animadversions so liberally advanced on the memory of a gallant General—slain on the plains of Waterloo!

It is apparent in the dispatch, that General Picton did report particularly the conduct of the officers in command of corps in his Division. And, it is also stated, that the Generals commanding Divisions had likewise commended the officers of those departments attached to them, although their names were not published. But, so numerous were recommendations, that it was, no doubt, difficult to make selections; which, it is presumed, was the cause of the applications in my favor by General Picton, Colonel Fletcher, Colonel Stewart, and others, being obscured in the multitude. However, I was soon afterwards appointed to a vacant company in my regiment, in the usual course. Nevertheless, as honor was my reward—which I am fully sensible of, and highly esteem—I cherish the hope of that honor being illumined by some token, in acknowledgement of my voluntary exertions and sufferings at Badajos: as also in Sir John Moore's retreat, and wound at the Battle of Corunna.

General Picton's friendly letters and kindness to me after his return from the Peninsula, and lastly on the morning previous his departure for Waterloo, are most gratefully esteemed by me as proofs of his estimation of my conduct, particularly, when he gave me his hand at parting as we walked together from his door, with this assurance, that 'I will not quit the Duke of Wellington without convincing him of your services.'
This is further evidence of General Picton's attention to the interests of those who had served under his command; and also of the natural amiableness of his noble disposition!

THE DEEDS HE DID, FAME DELIGHTS TO TELL,
AND MOCK OBLIVION'S POWER!
—AT WATERLOO HE FELL.

M.

1st July, 1836.

The Storming of Fort Napoleon, Almarez

THE Siege of Badajos having terminated by the capture of that powerful Fortress, with all its garrison, stores, &c., the Divisions of the enemy's army retired from Alentejo and Spanish Estremadura; the next object of the Earl of Wellington, was a considerable Fortification forming the grand pass, at Almarez, midway between Badajos and Madrid, eighty English miles from the former, ninety-six miles from the latter, thirty miles from Truxillo, and sixty miles from Merida, situated on the right bank of the Tagus; consisting of Fort Napoleon, strongly fortified, with double ditch, and armed with eighteen twenty-four pounders, and other ordnance; and connected by a floating bridge with a battery of six guns on the opposite side of the river, possessing a numerous garrison well supplied with all kinds of stores, and, being in the general route from the grand arsenal Seville, (via) Badajos, Truxillo, and Toledo, to Madrid, was an obstacle of immediate consideration, the destruction of which was confided to Lieut. General Sir Rowland Hill (now Lord Hill, Commanding-in-chief,) who marched his Division from Almandralejo to Merida and Truxillo, and issued orders for his 1st Brigade to attack Fort Napoleon by storm, on the night of the 18th or before daylight on the 19th of May, 1812.

The 2nd Brigade was directed to make a false attack on the front of a Castle, containing a small garrison, situated on the peak of a mountain (like a sugar-loaf) which was seated on the one side of the pass it formed on the main road from Truxillo, about four miles from Almarez, and a deep extensive wooded valley on the other side, while the 1st Brigade proceeded circuitously through the valley by the base of the mountain.

The 1st Brigade (50th, 71st, and 92nd regiments) was conducted by experienced guides in the mazy sheep-walks in the brushwood, which were considered impassable, and arrived near the Fort when the enemy had no suspicion of assailants in that direction. The march was consequently difficult, and so tedious, that the whole of the 50th regiment and the left wing of the 71st Light Infantry, only, were able to thread their way to Fort Napoleon by six o'clock in the morning of the 19th of May, when the sun was shining so resplendent, that as each individual emerged from the labyrinth he was distinguishable, and obliged to lay down (in ambush) to avoid discovery from the battlements; therefore Lieut. Colonel Stewart, (50th regiment) in command of the Brigade, obtained permission to attack Fort Napoleon with this portion only, in preference to the lapse of several hours in waiting the arrival of the remainder of the Brigade,—and knowing that his men would be discovered as soon as they stood up, the batteries open upon them, and numbers destroyed while instinctively discharging their firelocks at the enemy on the ramparts, he judiciously considered that the only plan was by a simultaneous rush to the wall, where the cannon had less effect, and then, instantly to escalade. He therefore gave strict orders that no man should load his musket until his arrival under the walls, and strongly recommended the use of the bayonet. Colonel Stewart had described in his regimental orders, previously, the use of the bayonet, and directed that time should not be wasted in the over application of the bayonet on any one individual a touch of a few inches being sufficient :—meaning, that equal justice should be administered to all opposers, by the compliment— 'en passant'—of the British bayonet only.

Our soldiers were formed for the assault in three Divisions, and advanced, preceded by the men bearing ladders, through the enemy's tremendous fire, instantly showered upon them, sweeping away all the which men carrying one ladder, but which was caught up and conveyed by others. Notwithstanding, all the ladders were immediately planted against the walls, but being rather short, exposed the escaladers to the rapid fire of the enemy's musketry within, while in the act of scrambling over the parapet; and Captain Candler (50th regiment) resolving to lead his company (as did all the officers) went first up his ladder, was pierced by several balls on the top of the wall and dropped dead inside. The escalade was not confined to the ladders only: our soldiers were impatient, and climbing dilapidated parts, pulled up their comrades, laid in the inner ditch till all were gathered, and then dashed forward—Colonel Stewart himself gallantly leading.

The assault was impetuous, and though the enemy continued to discharge from the twenty-four pounders grape and
round shot, and showers from musketry, our fellows, scampered
up the ladders and over the ramparts in defiance of the *desperate resistance*; which so astonished the enemy that the garrison
fled out of the Fort to the bridge, in order to gain the opposite battery, pursued by the British; but many of the French
who succeeded in passing over, recollecting—'self-preservation
to be nature's law,'—severed their end of the bridge to secure
themselves, which prevented even the chance of their own
comrades escape; these were forced again into the Fort by our
soldiers with the bayonet, and numbers of gallant defenders
were slaughtered, especially in the gateway, where the conflict
was severe. Those of the enemy who had escaped over and
broke the bridge, flew in desperation to the opposite battery
and fired indiscriminately into the Fort, the guns of which
were turned on that battery, which, with its magazine, was
entirely destroyed, with most of its defenders.

Thus, was Fort Napoleon possessed with all its ordnance,
stores, &c., and the garrison made prisoners, within half an hour.

The Governor' finding his strongly armed Fortress, with a
garrison of three thousand men, surprised and conquered so
instantaneously by a British regiment and a half about twelve
hundred men—became frantic, refusing to surrender his sword,
and flourishing it in defiance attempted' to strike an officer of
the 50th, who was remonstrating with him, when a sergeant, in
the warmth of the moment, unfortunately wounded him, with
his pike; which was deplored as unnecessary; because the poor
man with his whole garrison being absolutely prisoners of war,
his excitement must soon have subsided. Every assistance and

consolation were administered to him; but he, as also others of the wounded on both sides, after eight days' journey to Merida expired there.

In the Fort was a French artillery officer's wife; she was dressed in a kind of male attire, (as a personal security it was supposed,) but which was her equestrian costume, a travelling cap, pelisse, and Turkish trowsers, adapted for her mode of riding on horseback, (like a man,) to whom the British officers instantly gave protection; but, the soldiers in the first moments of victory having rummaged the apartments, she lost all her baggage and considerable property before the officers were aware of it; however, some of her wardrobe and other articles were collected and restored to her, but every endeavour to recover for her from the despoilers (amongst whom were some French soldiers) the whole of her property, was unsuccessful, although rewards were offered—and she quitted the Fort in grief, leaning on the arms of her husband and Captain Staple ton, 50th regiment. She was afterwards accommodated with a horse, and rode the remainder of the journey, accompanied by her husband. ·

The prisoners were sent off under the usual escort; and the conquerors bivouacked on the heights they had descended from in the morning, during the removal of the wounded—burying the dead—arranging transportable stores—and the demolition of the fortifications.

While the assault on Fort Napoleon was proceeding, the remainder of General Hill's Division possessed all the neighbourhood.

The right wing of the 71st Light Infantry, and the 92nd regiment (Highlanders,) were detached to carry the entrenched

houses at the bridge, and cut off the enemy's retreat; by proceeding circuitously they arrived, burned the bridge, destroyed
the temporary barracks, and joined in the general devastation,
the blowing up of the magazine, and the *entire destruction* of Fort
Napoleon, and the whole Grand Pass of Almarez: which being
completed, the Division returned to Merida, (via) Truxillo,
leaving the small Castle with its few soldiers destitute on the
mountain, and considered by the General not worth further
trouble. The poor devils remained as long as they could subsist,
and crept off towards their army, without the probability of
ever reaching it.

General Sir Rowland Hill embraced the earliest opportunity of expressing himself to all the officers, personally, and to
the men, generally, in terms of the highest approbation of their
conduct; which was repeated in general orders.

The loss of the 50th regiment in the assault of Fort Napoleon, 19th May, 1812.

KILLED.

1 Captain—Candler.—26 Rank and file.

WOUNDED.

1 Captain—Sandys, severely, since dead,
3 Lieuts.—Richardson, severely,
—— John Patterson, slightly,
—— Hemsworth, severely,
3 Ensigns—Godfrey, slightly
—— Crofton, slightly,
—— Goddard, -severely,

1 Sergeant Major—5 Sergeants—87 Rank and file.
Total 50th Regt. killed and wounded 126.

The loss of the left wing of 71st regiment was 1 Captain, severely wounded; and of other officers and rank and file, in proportion to the 50th;—the Captain survived only a few hours.

The Battle of Corunna

SIR JOHN MOORE'S Army was· intended (with the organization and co-operation of the national corps) to preserve Spain from the power of the French, and re-establish its tranquillity; but to such excess were the political jealousies, and intrigues of traitors to their own nation, that the schemes in progress for the absolute sale and delivery of Sir John Moore's Army, by the Spanish Patriots, into the hands of the French Invaders, were near completion, when General Moore's indefatigable penetration discovered that the pretended difficulties of the Juntas, their apprehensions, irresolutions, delays, and at last their total apathy, were designs, only to allure him. He, therefore, finding the Spanish Corps disbanded, and himself unsupported, determined on withdrawing his army towards his ships, and, from Spain, should the latter become his only alternative; and he commenced his retrograde in an acute angle, when on the march to Valladolid, and turned towards Corunna; this was instinctively discerned by the soldiers, sagaciously remarking after a night-march, that, 'the sun, yesterday morning, rose on our right-side; and this morning, it rises nearly on our left; —we must have made a sharp turn.'

Abandoned and deceived by our Spanish friends—to the utmost of their abilities-it became necessary for Sir John Moore to return to his ships. His masterly retreat in the midst of an inclement winter,—pressed by the overwhelming legions of Napoleon, and through unusual impediments of dilapidated towns, snow-covered mountains, craggy precipices, and deep rivers, the troops enduring severe fatigue and privations,—terminated by the glorious battle of Corunna.

On entering Corunna, 11th January, 1809, the narrator's regiment was quartered in a convent in the Citadel, where he was snugly lodged in a closet, and reposed comfortably upon a shelf, kindly permitting a friend to lay on another below him; and shutting the door, they were secure from intruders; with the luxury of putting off shoes only, (hourly expecting to 'fall in,') they soon forgot their late toils, in sound sleep.

The vessels which had been sent to Vigo were returning by express, when the enemy, having brought up his massive columns, formed his line in hostile array in a strong position on the high land which sloped to the village of Elvina, about two leagues from Corunna; menacing our defensive lines, posted in front to check his further advance; but the enemy continuing to display preparations for attack, General Moore presented his whole force in opposition, (all the troops having been previously marched out of Corunna,) and bivouacked in line on the high ground facing the enemy, having the village of Elvina in the valley, in front of the right of the British line, and nearly midway between the armies. The land, from the left of the enemy's line to the bottom of the declivity, was an inclined plane; and, from the right of the British line, the declivity was in steps of land, or flat fields successively below each other. On an angle of the lowest step stood the church, overlooking the village, the road to which wound round the base of the church, down the steep, and through the village to the extreme left of the enemy's line, from which returned a deep lane, skirting the village, and passing within a few yards of the church to the upland on the right of the British line. Between the church and the lane was the priest's house, from which was a path to the lane, through a gap in the bank. Beyond the village, on the right of the British line, but nearer to the enemy's left, was a house with a plantation, in which a picquet of Lord Bentinck's Brigade was placed.

On the morning of the 16th of January, 1809, the enemy having received considerable reinforcements, extended his line very considerably: and we were surprised by seeing a woman with a baby coming direct from the enemy's line to us. She was an Irishwoman, the wife of a soldier of the light com-pany of the 50th regiment, had lain-in on the march, was kindly attended by doctors of the French army, supported at the expense of Marshal Soult, arrived with his baggage, and was this morning sent over with Soult's compliments, that he should soon visit the 50th regiment. Soon after the arrival of this woman, our picquet was drove in, and a battery planted by the enemy at the house it had occupied. A couple of shots from a nine-pounder in our encampment were sent through the house, and made the fellows scamper out of it; and, as it was not considered necessary to discharge the gun again, the enemy expeditiously completed the battery and opened its fire, under cover of which the columns advanced in 'double quick' from their left to our right.

Lord William Bentinck's Brigade, 4th—50th—42nd regiments, being the right of the British line, was ordered to 'fall in.' The ensigns of the 50th regiment—Moore and Stewart—unfurled the colours by order of Major Napier; who, in allusion to Marshal Soult's message, bravely (enthusiastically) said, 'Open the colours that they may see the 50th!'—himself continuing in front, and the men remaining, sometime, with 'ordered arms,' loaded, as were the 4th and 42nd, as tranquilly as in a barrack-yard, viewing the enemy and waiting the attack. Several shots from the enemy's battery approached, and one entered the earth at the very toes of the right-centre company-to which the men involuntarily, but respectfully, formed a semicircle, the captain immediately gave the word 'dress!' and the men dressed up on the twirling shot. At this instant the enemy's Light Infantry approached very briskly (beaucoup de courage) within a few paces, firing, and wounded some men of the 50th as they stood like a wall in front of their encampment; but the whole Brigade then receiving the word 'forward,' advanced, firing and charging with the bayonet; few of the enemy's foremost escaped the punishment due to their temerity.

The 4th, or King's regiment, halted at the first step of land where an open front enabled them to mow the ranks of the attacking columns, with a steadiness and certainty that prevented the enemy's grand object of turning the right, and assured him that his design was impracticable—but the loss of the 4th regiment was very considerable.

The 42nd Highland regiment most judiciously took its position on the left of the village, so that the enemy's columns descending from the line, were not only exposed to the cross-fire of the 42nd and 4th regiments, but suffered very severely from the frequent charges with the bayonets of the brave Highlanders.

The 50th regiment had no other alternative than to pursue the Light Troops, and meet the enemy's columns in the village, which became the place of contention, and a most severe struggle ensued—the killed and wounded of the British and French soldiers fell upon each other-so personal was the contest. Here Major Stanhope was killed, and the ensigns Moore and Stewart mortally wounded, as was Lieut. Wilson, in advancing; he had been in extraordinary high spirits all the morning, and dressed himself in a new suit of regimentals, (preserved in the retreat,) 'to meet Master Smut,' as he expressed himself. Major Napier was missing, and supposed killed, some of the soldiers asserting that they saw him fall.—He was severely wounded and made prisoner;—he recovered and returned to England, in exchange.

When the 50th regiment rushed down from their camp, in pursuit, an officer seeing the church on an eminence over the turn of the road, as has been described, and supposing it to contain a body of the enemy in ambush; and beholding, also, the French rapidly filling the lane so contiguous, he considered it necessary to oppose them, and prevent the probability of their turning their fire on the rear of the 50th regiment, when the latter had passed. He, therefore, extending his arms, stopped several of his men, and having arranged them at the corner of the church, himself entered the church, which, however, was empty; but the priest's house, between the church and the lane, was full of French soldiers, from the lane. The officer came out, ran round and rejoined his men who, being screened by the angle of the church, kept up a brisk fire upon the enemy in the lane, and several times cleared the gap, where a French officer, rather below the middle stature, with stick in hand, exerted himself most gallantly to supply the gap; on which his men laid their firelocks, and killed two and wounded three of this little band; but fortunately the British officer had picked up a dragoon carabine on the road near Corunna, which he retained as a 'Friend in need.' This he had previously loaded with two small buttons from the collar of his regimental coat, and having been supplied with French cartridges at the church, he was enabled to assist his men by discharging his carabine many times in defence of his post; and the French officer at the gap seeming resolved to force his way at the head of his men, the dragoon carabine rested against the corner of the church ensured an aim which *for ever checked his progress*, and his men drew back. 'The defenders of the church' with their officer immediately made a dash at the priest's house, and the enemy—upwards of twenty—within it, rushed out, but not being able to reach the gap, turned suddenly round, and instead of cutting off the church party, fled into the house, slapped the door, and fired at random out of the windows, which afforded the church party an opportunity of retiring from their hazardous attempt.

About this time General Moore was mortally wounded on a rising ground behind the right flank of the 42nd regiment, overlooking the village and the enemy's columns, and upon an elevation equal to the French battery, His absence from that spot was noticed, but it was not then known that he had fallen.

There is no doubt but the French supposed that a very considerable party of the 50th was in ambush behind the church; and, therefore, unable to penetrate at that point, pushed up the lane to assist in gaining the right of the 4th regiment, but there they were warmly repulsed, and outflanked by the brave rifle corps, from whom they suffered severely.

Sixty rounds of fresh ammunition, and an extra bundle of ten (the latter the men put into their pockets) were previously issued to the Brigade, but the 50th regiment having expended all their ammunition and what they had collected from their fallen comrades and the enemy, and being too far advanced to receive a supply, was obliged to retire on the step of land above the church, facing outwards and parallel to the lane. Here they became a barrier—sustaining the enemy's fire—and making arrangements for maintaining their position with the bayonet, kept the enemy at bay—without being possessed of a single cartridge—although nearly all the left wing of the regiment was exposed to the enemy, and occasioned the adoption of the 'kneeling position' firelocks in hand, for some time; but, as many of the men (towards the left) were shot in the head and fell dead, the soldiers were obliged to prostrate themselves with their muskets in their grasp—anxiously waiting the return of messengers for ammunition. This situation the regiment maintained some time, (and growing dusk,) when the 'Guards' advanced, but mistaking the orders, halted on the step of land above, and called to the 50th regiment that they were come to support them, when several distant voices exclaimed 'no, relieve the 50th.' The Rifles were sharply engaged at this time in the front. The Guards instantly advanced deploying on their right, to take up the same ground; but the leading—if he survives—will remember approaching a wounded officer and another who sat by him, and was requested by them to file considerably to his right, or more than half of his regiment would be thrown into the enemy's fire, before their line could be formed.

The loss of the 42nd and 50th regiments were nearly equal, and very severe. Several men of the 50th, who volunteered from the French 70th regiment at Vimeira, were here killed in the ranks of the 50th regiment. Major Campbell 42nd regiment, died of fatigue on his arrival at Plymouth.

The 50th regiment retired to their former camp-ground, where Captain Armstrong had borne the corpse of Major Stanhope and laid him at his great length; he was very tall and slim, (resembling in person his relation Mr. Pitt,) and much esteemed and lamented. He was there interred. Ammunition arrived, and the men prepared to rejoin the combat, but the enemy having been completely repelled on the right, next aimed at the centre, and there likewise repulsed, made a third assault on the left, which was continued to a village on the high road, and like Elvina, became the 'scene of another desperate struggle, which was gallantly sustained by the 14th Regiment, and the enemy completely vanquished.

Night veiled the combatants, and the enemy withdrew leaving the British line considerably advanced: meditating, no doubt, to retrieve the last defeat of columns by a more powerful assault supported by reinforcements.

During the night of the 16th of January, the embarkation of the remains of the army of the lamented Sir John Moore commenced, except the Brigades of Generals Hill and Beresford, which continued on the Heights; and these were embarked on the 17th, as were all that could be collected as long as the boats could be used; but numbers of men, women, and children, lined the shore opposite the Castle when the fleet departed, amongst whom was a Grenadier officer of the 81st regiment severely wounded, laid by his men upon the shingle, to seek their own safety.

The officer (of the carabine) having been wounded in the left thigh by a man who fired at him twice in the same direction, was more fortunate; he had been conveyed in a waggon, with others, to a convent in the Citadel, and in the morning crawled down to the beach, where he was immediately surrounded by many men of his regiment, amongst whom was his own servant. The greetings of master and man were naturally Interesting—'How are you?' and, 'How are you, Sir?' The servant had two shots in his shoulder, and arm shattered. All were now dependent on their own exertions, and the officer, after several attempts, having thrown himself upon the edge of the last boat, (a last effort,) was dragged in by the collar, and with others placed safely on board a ship.

The enemy finding the British embarked, advanced, established a battery to command the harbour, and opened its fire, as the ships were getting under-weigh, on those which had not cleared out, and upon a particular transport, which had hitched on a point of rock; but the heavy guns of our men-of-war kept the battery in check, and the men from the damaged transport were removed to another.

A fair wind springing up, the whole of the British fleet quitted the harbour, but with longing, lingering looks, for those left behind on the road unable to reach Corunna—on the field of battle—the gallant Chief in his tomb—and those on the shore, whose hearts palpitating at our departure, sunk in their bosoms as the fleet sunk in the distance from their view.

The loss of the 50th regiment in the battle of Corunna, of the rank and file, could not be accurately ascertained, but the following is the list of officers:

KILLED.

Major Stanhope-Lieut. Wilson,
Ensign Moore, Bearing the Colours
Ensign Stewart, Bearing the Colours

WOUNDED.

Major Napier, severely,—prisoner,
Captain Clunes, slightly,
Captain Armstrong, slightly,
Lieut. Macdonald, slightly,
Lieut. Mac Carthy, severely.

FINIS.

Appendix

BADAJOS.

    NOTE p. 176. Thomas Martin, Esq. of Ballinaherd Castle, M. P., most nobly and gallantly served as a volunteer at the Siege of Badajos, having declined a commission offered him by Lord Berresford. In a letter to the author, Mr. Martin says, 'I was a volunteer with the storming party of the 88th regiment, on the night the Castle was taken by the 3rd Division, and was wounded as I was about to mount a ladder; and I shall ever consider that having served as a volunteer on that memorable night, has been the proudest action of my life.'

    NOTE p. 177. The attack and possession of the Castle, preceded that of the Town, 'and enabled the other Divisions, which had been powerfully resisted, to enter the Town;' and in consequence of the ladders of the 5th Division not arriving at the time appointed, (p. 39,) the assault by General Walker's Brigade was later than intended, and considerable loss sustained.

General Walker having found it advantageous, made a *real attack*, and himself leading with extraordinary gallantry,—which could not be exceeded,—his Brigade descended into the ditch, and as stated, (p. 177), escaladed the face of the bastion of St. Vincent, and gained the ramparts, although the ladders (conducted by a party under Major Faunce, 4th regiment) being too short, did not reach the top of the wall, and the men were obliged to push and pull each other up ; but an embrasure, without a gun was discovered in the curtain of the wall, by which many officers and men entered. Lieut. Stavely, 4th regiment, was killed on the top of a ladder, and numerous brave assailants fell.

The Brigade was ordered to man the ramparts, and the struggle was severe; when as General Walker was bravely leading his Brigade towards the interior of the breaches, to drive the enemy from thence, he received a most dangerous wound (p. 184) from a ball which struck him on the right side, breaking several ribs and driving in a part of the watch he carried in a small pocket in the breast of his coat. The Brigade continued its progress along the rampart, and the General was alone on the ground. Sometime after, a French soldier came to the spot, to whom General Walker said, 'I am an English General Officer, badly wounded, and if you will stay by me until you can find assistance to remove me into a house, I will reward you.' The soldier replied, 'Si vous êtes Général, vous avez des epaulettes, et de l'argent aussi sans doute.'—He then tore off the General's epaulettes, rifled his pockets, and left him. Afterwards, another French soldier approached, to him the General said, 'I have just been plundered by one of your comrades, and therefore have nothing to offer you now; but if you will stay by me till some one will assist you to carry me to a house, I will reward you. The man looked sternly at the General in his agony, without replying, and began to load his musket, the contents of which the General had no doubt, were intended for him; but when he had loaded, he said that he would remain with him; and soon after an English soldier came, and the two, the English and French soldier, carried the General to the French hospital, whence he was removed to a private house.

ALMAREZ.

NOTE p. 192. The elegant military cap of the French Commandant of Fort Napoleon, Almarez, was constantly worn, afterwards, as a trophy by the drum-major of the 50th regiment.

CORUNNA.

NOTE p. 202. It is probable, that Lord William Bentinck, commanding the Brigade, saw from the position he was in, the exertions of the officer with the carabine and his party at the corner of the church, (which may recur to his Lordship's memory,) when the enemy

'Like waves that follow o'er the sea,
'Came thickly thundering on.'

Opposite: Casualty list from the 1836 edition of Captain MacCarthy's memoir.

RETURN OF KILLED AND WOUNDED

Of the Army under the command of His Excellency General The Earl of Wellington, at the storming of Badajos, 6 to 7 April, 1812.

KILLED.

Artil. Captain Latham—8 rank and file

Eng. Lieuts. Lacelles—De Salubury

Bn. Rgt.

1— 4 Captain Bellingham— lieut. Stavely—2 serj. —28 rank and file

2— 5 Major Ridge—1 serj.— 10 rank and file

1—7 Major Singer—capt. Cholwick—lieuts. Ray, Fowler, Pike—2 serj.—42 rank and file

1—23 Capt. Maw—lieut. Collins 3 serj.—19 rank & file

3—27 Capt. Jones—lieuts. Levinge, Simcoe, Whyte, —3 serj.—35 rank and

28 Capt. Johnson, A.D.C. to Major-Gen. Bowes

2—38 Ensign Evans—1 serj.— 11 rank and file

1—40 Lieuts. Greenshields, Ayling—volun. O'Brien— 5 serj.—46 rank and file

42 Capt. Munro

1—43 Lieut.-Col. McLeod— lieuts. Harvest, Taggart. 3 serj.—71 rank & file

2—44 Lieuts. Unthank, Argent —2 serj.—35 rank and file

1—45 Capt. Herrick — ensigns McDonnell, Collins— 1 serj.—18 rank & file

KILLED.

Bn. Rgt.

1—48 Capt. Brooke—lieut. Chiliot—ensign Barker— 3 serj.—29 rank & file

1—52 Capts. Jones, Madden, Poole — lieuts. Booth, Royle — 3 serj. — 50 rank and file

5—60 Lieut. Sterne—4 rank & file

2—83 Capt. Fry—1 serj.—22 rank and file

1—88 Capt. Lindsey — lieuts. Mansfield, McAlpin— 4 serj.—25 rank & file

94 Ens. Long—12 rank and file

1—95 Maj. O'Hare—Capt. Diggle— lieut. Stokes—3 serjeants—24 rank and file

Rifles

3—95 Lieuts. Hovenden, Cary, Allex, Crondace — 9 rank and file

Brunk. 7 rank and file

Portuguese.

3d line Lieut. de Silviera

11 — Lieut.-Col. McDonnell,— (91st British)

23 — Ensign de Cavallo

1stCac. Lieut. St. Valez

3 — Capt. Morphew (R.W.I.R. British)

8 — Capt. Bruning (Y.L.I. British)—Lieut. Pinta de Lousac

Rgt.	WOUNDED.
	GENERAL STAFF.
77	Lieut.-Gen. Sir Thomas Picton, slightly—Major Gen. Hon. C. Colville, severely
81	Maj. Gen. Kempt, slightly
50	Maj. Gen. Walker, dangerously
6	Maj. Gen. Bowes, severely
7 W.I.	Major Hon. H. Pakenham, asst. adj. gen., severely —Majors Brooke, Perm, asst. q. m. gen., severely
81	Capt. James, D. asst. adj. gen., severely
92	Brig. major McPherson, severely
28	Brig. maj. (capt.) Potter, severely
45	Brig. maj. (capt.) Campbell slightly
30	Brig. maj. (capt.) Machell, severely
71	Captain Spottiswoode, A. D. C. to major-gen. Colville, severely
5	Capt. Bennet, A. D. C. to gen. Kempt, severely
50	Lieut. Johnstone, A. D. C. to gen. Walker, slightly
Hus. 18	Lieut. Harris, A. D. C. to gen. Stewart, slightly

Rgt.	WOUNDED.
Rl. Art.	12 rank and file
R. Eng.	Capts. Nicholas, Williams —lieut. Emmett, severely—5 rank and file
K.G.A.	Lieut. Gochen, severely
1 Royal	Lieuts. Rae, McNail, acting Engineers, slightly
1— 4	Major Faunce, slightly—capts. Williamson, Wilson, Burke, Hanwell, severely—lieuts. Salvin,

Bn. Rgt.	WOUNDED.
	Convey, Boyd, slightly, Dean, Brown, Sheppard, Craster, Aley, severely —ens. Rawlins, Arnold, severely —8 serj.—1 d. 164 rank & file
2— 5	Capt. Doyle—lieut. J. Pennington—ens. Hopkins, severely—3 serj.—1 d. 26 rank and file
1— 7	Lieut.-colonel Blakeney—capt. Mair—lieuts. St. Pol, Moses, Devey, Barrington, Lester, Russell, George, severely; Henry, Baldwin, Knowles, slightly—11 serj.—108 rank and file
1—23	Capts. Leckey, Stainforth, sevrly.; Hawtyn, sltly. —lieuts. Johnson, Harrison, Tucker, G. Brown, Farmer, Walker, Brownson, Fielding, Whaley, Holmes, Winyates, Llewelyn, severely—7 serj. —1 d.—84 rank & file —1 serj. and 19 rank & file missing
3—27	Major Erskine (L.C.) severely — captain Ward (L. C.) ditto — lieuts. Thompson, Ratcliffe, severely; Gordon, Moore, Hanbey, Pollock, Weir, slightly—adj. Davidson, severely — ens. Warrington, ditto, died—9 serj.—123 rank & file
2—30	Major Grey (L.C.) sevrly died — capts. Hitchin, slightly; Chambers, severely — lieuts. Baillie,

WOUNDED.

Bn. Rgt.

Neville, slightly—ens.
Pratt, slightly—6 serj.
—82 rank and file

2—38 Capt. Barnard, severely—
lieuts. Magill, Lawrence,
severely — ens. Reed,
severely—1 serj.—1 d.
28 rank and file

1—40 Lieut.-colonel Harcourt—
maj. Gillies — captains
Phillips, sevrly; Bowen,
slightly—lieuts. Street,
Grey, Moore, Turton,
Butler, Millar, Anthony,
Toole, severely; Gor-
man, slightly — ensign
Johnson, sevrly. volun-
teer Widenham, ditto—
11 serj.—162 rank & file

1—43 Major Wells, severely—
capts. Ferguson, Stroud,
slightly—lieuts. Pollock
Rideout, Capell, W.
Freer, (right arm am-
putated) Oglander (left
arm amputated), Mad-
den, E. Freer, Consa-
dine, Bailie, severely;
Hodgson, O'Connell,
Cook, slightly—16 serj.
1 d.—238 rank & file

2—44 Lieut.-col. H. G. Carlton,
severely — capts. Ber-
wick, Brugh, Jervoise,
severely—lieuts. Mead,
slightly; Sinclair, se-
verely — ens. O'Reilly,
slightly—1 serj.—1 d.
—80 rank and file

1—45 Capts. Lightfoot, Flaharty,
slightly—lieuts. Powell,
Reynett, Metcalfe, se-
verely; McPherson,

WOUNDED.

Bn. Rgt

Dale, Monroe, slightly
—ens. Stewart, slightly
Jones, severely — vol.
Percy, ditto—8 serj.—
1 d.—55 rank & file

1—48 Lieut.-col. Erskine, severely—major Wilson,
ditto—capts. Bell, Turn-
penny, slightly; French,
severely—lieuts. Brook,
severely; Stroud, Cuth-
bertson, Robinson, Arm-
strong, Wilson, Pount-
ney, slightly—ensigns
Thatcher, Johnson,
Bourke, Thompson, slt.
—6 serj.—116 rank &
file

1—50 Lieut. MacCarthy, asst.-
engineer, severely

1—52 Lieut.-col. Gibbs, severely
—maj. Mein, ditto—
captains R. Campbell,
ditto, Merry, ditto, died
—lieuts. McNair, Kin-
lock, York, Davis, Royds,
slightly; Blackwood,
Barlow, C. Dawson,
severely—ens. Gawler,
slightly—adj. Winter-
bottom, ditto—18 serj.
234 rank and file

5—60 Lieut.-cols. Williams, Fitz-
gerald, slightly —lieut.
Gilse, ditto—adj. Bro-
ety, leg amptd., died—
2 serj.—24 rank & file

74 Lieut.-col. Hon. P. French
severely—capts. Lang-
lands, severely; Thomp-
son, slightly — lieuts.
Grant, King, severely;
Pattison, Ironside, slty.

WOUNDED.			WOUNDED.		
Bn.	Rgt.		Bn.	Rgt.	
		—3 serj.—30 rank and file—2 rank and file missing			(44 Brit.) brig.-major, severely—lieut. Alvaro di Costa, A. D. C. to gen. Harvey, severely —majs. Tullock, (Brit. artil.,) Anderson, (42 Brit.,) severely—capts. J. de Mattos, severely; F. de Almeida, J. Maria, slightly — lieuts. de la Serda, ditto; Clements, Pinto, dos Santos Cebral, severely—ens. Gonoon, Tavary, Oliva, d'Alverida, severely; Gos. Bernido, slightly
	77	Lieut.-col. Duncan, sltly.— lieuts. Clarke, severely; Pennefather, slightly— adj. Jones, slightly— 2 serg.—8 rank & file			
2	83	Lieuts. Bowles, O'Neil, Bloomfield, severely; Barry, FitzGibbon, slt.; ens. Vavasour, Lane, ditto—vol. Illera, ditto. 3 serj.—36 rank & file			
1	88	Capts. Murphy, (m.) sev. Peshall, sltly.—lieuts. Davern, sltly. Cockburn, Whitelaw, sev. Stewart, sev. died—ens. Grattan, sevrly.—9 serg.—1 d. 96 rank and file		15	Capt. T. O'Neil (32 Brit.) severely —ens. Poulal, severely
	92	Lieut. Cattenaugh, acting eng., slightly		21	Lieut Peruva, severely
	94	Lieut. Bogue, severely— 6 serj.—46 rank & file		23	Capt. R. Felix, slightly— lieuts. Rebocho, Madieras, ditto — ens. Mendorca, slightly; Pedro Retocho, Servieca, sev.
1	95	Captains Crampton, Balvaired, Grey, McDermid, slightly — lieuts. Johnson, Gardiner, Manners, McPherson, Forster, severely; Fitzmaurice, slightly — 15 serj.—3 d. — 136 rank and file	Caca.	1	Maj. Algeo (34 British) severely—captain Mac Donald, (71 Brit.) ditto ens. Rebello, ditto
Rifles.				3	Lieut.-col. Elder, (95 Br.) —major de Selviera— capts. Ignacio, Dobbin, (27 Br.)—lieuts. Paxato D'Ainderido—ens. Fexeira, severely
3	95	Lieuts. McDonald, Worsley, Stewart, severely; Farmer, slightly—vol. Lawson, ditto—2 serj. 45 rank and file		6	Captain O'Hara (47 Br.) slightly — lieuts. Camancho, sev; Graves, slightly—ens. Jose de Almeida, ditto
Brunsk.		Capt. Girswald, severely —lieut. Kunowskey, slt.		8	Capt. Magelaens, sev.— lieut. Condose, slightly ens. Lecha, ditto
Portug.		Br.-gen. Harvey (79 Brit.) severely—capt. Peacock			

Postscript

Copy of General Sir Thomas Picton's reply to
the private letter alluded to in the 'Address.'

Glamorganshire, 4th Nov., 1812.

My Dear Sir,
Your letter of the 27th ult. reached me in this Country.
I shall be in London early in December, when I shall have great
satisfaction in giving your claims every support in my power .
Your very faithful humble Servant,
THOS. PICTON.

Lieut. Mac Carthy, 50th Regt.

Franked,   Cardiff, Nov. 6th, 1812.
                 Lieut. Mac Carthy,

                                        50th Regt.
                                        Lewes,
                                        Sussex

Free,
Thos. Wyndham.

Index